MW01224722

OUT OF AFRICA

The Church of Nigeria possesses certain keys that will benefit the Church worldwide. Through my many visits to West Africa and through the ministering of the Nigerian apostles in our local assembly, I have personally benefited from the grace given to Nigerians. *Out of Africa* will stir you to become a carrier of God's glory. If God can bring revival to Nigeria, revival can come to any nation. I recommend *Out of Africa* to leaders and believers around the world.

APOSTLE JOHN ECKHARDT
IMPACT NETWORK OF CHURCHES

Wow! I just read *Out of Africa* and highly recommend it. Having been to Nigeria under the auspices of International Coalition of Apostles (ICA), I can say my eyes have seen the glory! This book is full of wisdom, knowledge, revelation and much information. It gives great insight to what the Lord is saying and doing in the Church, even beyond Nigeria. Once you start reading *Out of Africa,* you can't put it down!

APOSTLE JOHN P. KELLY
PRESIDENT, LEADERSHIP EDUCATION FOR APOSTOLIC DEVELOPMENT
AMBASSADOR APOSTLE, ICA

When I visited Nigeria, I had been battling sickness for several years. I came home healed. There is a huge anointing on the Church in Nigeria. God's people are on fire there. As you read *Out of Africa,* catch the fire of God that is spreading across Nigeria and release it in your region!

CHUCK D. PIERCE
COAUTHOR, *RESTORING YOUR SHIELD OF FAITH*
VICE PRESIDENT, GLOBAL HARVEST MINISTRIES
PRESIDENT, GLORY OF ZION INTERNATIONAL

C. PETER WAGNER

General Editor

OUT OF AFRICA

JOSEPH THOMPSON

General Editor

Regal

From Gospel Light
Ventura, California, U.S.A.

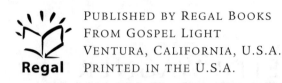

PUBLISHED BY REGAL BOOKS
FROM GOSPEL LIGHT
VENTURA, CALIFORNIA, U.S.A.
PRINTED IN THE U.S.A.

Regal Books is a ministry of Gospel Light, an evangelical Christian publisher dedicated to serving the local church. We believe God's vision for Gospel Light is to provide church leaders with biblical, user-friendly materials that will help them evangelize, disciple and minister to children, youth and families.

It is our prayer that this Regal book will help you discover biblical truth for your own life and help you meet the needs of others. May God richly bless you.

For a free catalog of resources from Regal Books/Gospel Light, please call your Christian supplier or contact us at 1-800-4-GOSPEL *or* www.regalbooks.com.

All Scripture quotations, unless otherwise indicated, are taken from the *New King James Version.* Copyright © 1979, 1980, 1982 by Thomas Nelson, Inc. Used by permission. All rights reserved.

Other versions used are
KJV—King James Version. Authorized King James Version.
NIV—Scripture taken from the *Holy Bible, New International Version®.* Copyright © 1973, 1978, 1984 by International Bible Society. Used by permission of Zondervan Publishing House. All rights reserved.
NLT—Scripture quotations marked *(NLT)* are taken from the *Holy Bible,* New Living Translation, copyright © 1996. Used by permission of Tyndale House Publishers, Inc., Wheaton, Illinois 60189. All rights reserved.
TEV—Scripture quotations are from *Today's English Version.* Copyright © American Bible Society 1966, 1971, 1976. Used by permission.

© 2004 C. Peter Wagner and Joseph Thompson
All rights reserved.

Cover and interior design by Robert Williams
Edited by Stephanie Parrish

Library of Congress Cataloging-in-Publication Data
Out of Africa / edited by C. Peter Wagner and Joseph Thompson.
    p. cm.
Includes bibliographical references.
  ISBN 0-8307-3292-6
  1. Church growth—Nigeria. 2. Nigeria—Church history. I. Wagner, C.
Peter. II. Thompson, Joseph, 1963–
  BR1463.N5O88 2003
  276.69'083—dc22   2003021098

2 3 4 5 6 7 8 9 10 11 12 13 14 15 / 09 08 07 06 05 04

Rights for publishing this book in other languages are contracted by Gospel Light Worldwide, the international nonprofit ministry of Gospel Light. Gospel Light Worldwide also provides publishing and technical assistance to international publishers dedicated to producing Sunday School and Vacation Bible School curricula and books in the languages of the world. For additional information, visit www.gospellightworldwide.org; write to Gospel Light Worldwide, P.O. Box 3875, Ventura, CA 93006; or send an e-mail to info@gospellightworldwide.org.

CONTENTS

INTRODUCTION

C. Peter Wagner

C. Peter Wagner serves as president of Global Harvest Ministries, based in Colorado Springs, Colorado. He is also chancellor of Wagner Leadership Institute and presiding apostle of the International Coalition of Apostles. Known by many for his teaching gift, he has taught for over 30 years as professor of church growth at Fuller Theological Seminary.

Wagner is a prolific author, having published over 60 books on subjects such as missions, church growth, spiritual gifts, leadership, healing, spiritual warfare, revival, Christian character and apostolic ministries. His commentary on the book of Acts, Acts of the Holy Spirit, is his favorite title.

He, along with his wife, Doris, served as field missionaries in Bolivia for 16 years. They have three daughters, who have given them nine grandchildren.

Nigeria is known by many as the Giant of Africa. The nation is roughly two and one-half times the size of Texas. Its population of somewhere between 140 million and 160 million constitutes half of Africa's people. One out of every five black persons in the world lives in Nigeria. Furthermore, an estimated 40 million Nigerians now reside in other countries of the world, including the United States.

Nigeria is also a giant of today's Christian landscape. I say "a" giant rather than "the" giant because Mainland China may rival Nigeria as the epicenter of Christian power in the world today. Having said that, of all the countries to which we have free access, I would place Nigeria atop the list of those with a dynamic explosion of the Christian faith in our times.

A NEW MISSION FIELD

Our old stereotype of Africa as "the mission field" has long since become antiquated. To the contrary, we here in the West could only wish that the supernatural power of God so plainly evident there could, at least to some degree, penetrate our jaded post-Christian society. In Africa, every day sees 24,500 new Christian church members, according to David B. Barrett and Todd M. Johnson, coeditors of *World Christian Trends Encyclopedia* and coauthors of *World Christian Trends*.[1] Compare this to 5,000 in North America. Of the six continents of the world, Africa is currently experiencing the most accelerated rate of church growth at 2.62 percent per year. Asia (including China) is second with 2.12 percent. As a point of contrast, we here in North America are seeing only 0.81 percent annual growth.[2]

What does this mean? It means that the tables have turned. Instead of Africa's being the mission field needing American missionaries, America is now the mission field needing African missionaries. Indeed, one African church, the Redeemed Christian Church of God (RCCG), is one of numerous African churches currently sending missionaries to America. At this writing the RCCG has planted over 150 churches in America, many of which have over 500 members. Since we are talking numbers, keep in mind that 90 percent of American churches have 200 or fewer members.

THE SHIFT IN CHURCH GROWTH

During the 1970s and 1980s, the most dramatic church growth in the world was taking place in South Korea. At that time, no one thought that a Methodist church could grow to 80,000 members, but Bishop Kim Sundo proved that it could happen. In fact, Kim became so influential that he was elected president of the worldwide association of Methodist bishops. Pastor David Yonggi Cho had his sights set even higher. At the peak of his Full Gospel Church, he reported 750,000 members; and when he constructed an auditorium to seat 25,000, the rest of the world stood in awe.

With all of this, God has His times and seasons. Due to a number of factors, the growth of South Korean churches slowed down and plateaued in 1990. At that time the Christian population of South Korea had risen rapidly from practically zero to 25 percent of the total population. If the same rate of growth had continued, South Korean Christians today would represent nearly 40 percent of the nation's population. Regrettably, the figure has remained at only 25 percent—just what it was 10 years ago.

However, this book is not about Korea but about Nigeria. My personal assessment of the situation is that the same hand of God that was on South Korea during its period of explosive growth began to shift to Nigeria during the 1990s. Today

Nigeria can be considered the center of gravity as far as the dramatic, visible, outward manifestation of the presence of the kingdom of God is concerned.

Let's take a brief look at what God is doing in Nigeria.

Deeper Life Bible Church

I began to suspect that something extraordinary was going on in Nigeria in the early 1990s when I was invited by Pastor William Kumuyi to train leaders in a pastors' conference that he would convene. I was stunned when I saw the crowd of 13,000 pastors and leaders who had registered for the conference. In fact, Kumuyi had constructed a building to hold that many people just for the conference. It was so new when I arrived that the plaster was still wet on some of the walls.

Kumuyi invited me to speak to his Deeper Life Bible Church headquarters congregation on Sunday. The Sunday attendance at that time was 74,000 adults, with 40,000 children in the building across the street. The last I heard, that local church has 150,000 members. Kumuyi has planted more than 5,000 Deeper Life Bible Churches across Nigeria and has sent church-planting missionaries to start Deeper Life movements in virtually every other African nation, as well as many nations outside of Africa. Little wonder that he could announce the conference and see 13,000 pastors come to his retreat center near Lagos for training.

The Nigerian Apostolic Summit

Ten years later I revisited Nigeria. This time, with the help of my fellow apostle Joseph Thompson, coeditor of this book, I convened a Nigerian Apostolic Summit under the auspices of the International Coalition of Apostles. Meeting with those Nigerian apostles was a remarkable experience. Four of the five most prominent Nigerian apostles attended (William Kumuyi could not make it), as well as many others. All four have written stimulating chapters in this book. Before the meeting ended, I realized that I was in the presence of unusually gifted servants of God. Let me make a rather bold statement: These four apostles seated together in that room constituted the most powerful coalition of anointed Christian leadership in one place that I had ever seen. (Incidentally, they do not as yet feel comfortable using the title "apostle," although they fully recognize their apostolic role.)

No wonder Joseph Thompson and I decided on the spot that these leaders had something extremely important to share with American believers. That is how the book that you now have in your hands, *Out of Africa*, was born.

Winners Chapel
One of the four leading apostles, Bishop David Oyedepo, the author of chapter 10, agreed to host the apostolic summit. He generously took care of all the accommodations and food. It was an unforgettable experience when we, after fighting traffic for two hours on the chaotic streets of Lagos and then through the suburb of Ota, entered the gate of Canaan Land, as Oyedepo calls his campus. In an instant we had gone from chaos to peace. Canaan Land spans more than 630 acres of land. Half of the campus houses the church, Winners Chapel, and the other half is the site of Covenant University.

Winners Chapel auditorium, also called Faith Tabernacle, is the largest church building in the world. It contains 50,400 chairs—comfortable white plastic deck chairs with arms. This is over twice the capacity of Cho's building in Korea. The choir loft accommodates 1,000 people. Each of the three major wings of the auditorium is the size of two football fields. Surrounding the auditorium are office buildings, faculty housing, classrooms for a K-12 school, a church-owned shopping center containing everything from fast food to a bank, a fleet of 200 perfectly matched buses imported from America, spacious guest houses, a chapel that seats 3,000, Sunday School rooms, and more. It is the first church I ever attended that owns a full-service gas station.

We were privileged to attend Winners Chapel's Thursday night prayer and communion service, which runs from 5:00 to 8:00 P.M. Three thousand congregants packed the chapel, while another 3,000 participated through live television transmission in other meeting rooms. I never thought I would see a local church weeknight prayer meeting with 6,000 people in attendance.

Bishop Oyedepo told me that Winners Chapel campus had cost the equivalent of $250 million. It was all Nigerian money—nothing from the outside. When I asked him how he could get that much money, he told me that it was very simple: Everyone in his church tithes. He teaches them biblical prosperity: God keeps His promise; if they give, it will be given back with an overflowing measure. He instructs them not only to tithe the first 10 percent but also to save the next 10 percent. That is the reason the church started a bank. As they have obeyed God and their pastor, thousands of members of Winners Chapel have been lifted from poverty to the newly emerging Nigerian middle class.

This is to say nothing about Covenant University, already chartered by the Nigerian government. When I was there, it was under construction on the other half of the Canaan Land campus. No fewer than 1,400 construction workers were working in shifts 24 hours a day. Before this book is out on the shelves, Covenant University will be open to accommodate 6,500 resident students from all over Africa, grounding them in the righteous and just principles of the kingdom of God. My friends and I were invited to pray a prayer of dedication in the unfinished dining hall, which is designed to seat 3,500 at once. Oyedepo told us that this will cost another $250 million and that the money is already in the bank. Covenant University will be dedicated debt free.

All-Night Prayer Meeting

On the first Friday of every month, the Redeemed Christian Church of God holds an all-night prayer meeting at Redemption Campground. We were invited to attend the prayer meeting as personal guests of General Overseer Enoch A. Adeboye. When our group arrived there to join the prayer meeting, we could not believe our eyes. We were in the midst of no fewer than 500,000 believers who had come to pray all night long! Since I was hearing conflicting figures, I decided to pace off the building the next morning to see for myself how big it was. The building currently is the size of 69 football fields! When the roof is completed, it could contain 86 football fields.

We measured Redemption Campground itself using our automobile odometer—it is 0.65 square miles. The platform itself seats over 4,500 persons. Every December, reportedly between 6 and 7 million persons attend the RCCG Holy Ghost Congress.

City of David

Nigeria is a poor nation with a very small middle class. However, some Nigerians are rich. Many of them live on Victoria Island, which is like the Beverly Hills of Lagos. I was invited by Pastor Eskor Mfon to minister in his church, City of David (an RCCG church), on Victoria Island. It is a church of 2,500 people who meet in a restaurant facility, which they fill twice every Sunday. Most church members are business executives, military officers and government officials. Mfon, whose story you will love reading in chapter 11, showed me a new building under construction that will seat 3,000. "This is our future youth center," he said. "Our sanctuary will be much larger."

Among other things, City of David furnishes a hot meal every Sunday for 30,000 poor people in Lagos. Joining with Joe Olaiya, who has written chapter 5, a powerful chapter on prayer, City of David provides an additional 5,000 meals every Sunday in the Muslim area of northern Nigeria. For most of these people, this is the only square meal they can plan on in a given week. Is Mfon satisfied? No. Here's what he says: "We are feeding people one day a week, but with God on our side and more funds, we shall be able to feed every day!"

WORLD MISSIONS

Nigeria is now becoming known as one of the great missionary-sending nations of the world. For example, two of the three largest churches in Europe today were planted by Nigerian missionaries. Wait until you read the thrilling chapter by Sunday Adelaja who went to Kiev, Ukraine, on a Communist-funded scholarship, only to end up pastoring a church of over 20,000, the largest church in Europe. He has planted over 100 additional churches in the Ukraine, 19 in Russia, 12 in former USSR nations, plus churches in Israel, Germany, the United States, United Arab Emirates and the Netherlands. Adelaja trained an apostolic leadership team of 12 apostles, whom he sent out to the nations to minister. He now has a second group of 12, whom he is training to be missionaries.

I already mentioned that the Redeemed Christian Church of God has 150 churches in America and counting. Enoch Adeboye estimates that they are planting between 5 and 10 new RCCG churches every day in Nigeria and around the world. At last count they have over 6,000 churches in more than 50 nations of the world. Mike Okonkwo, bishop of the Redeemed Evangelical Mission in Lagos, Nigeria, also has numerous church plants around Europe.

Some of the largest churches in Italy, Jamaica, Ghana and various other nations were all planted and are pastored by

> *I wouldn't be at all surprised if more new churches were being planted by Nigerians outside of their own country than by Americans outside of theirs.*

Nigerian missionaries. And I wouldn't be at all surprised if more new churches were being planted by Nigerians outside of their own country than by Americans outside of theirs.

SIGNS AND WONDERS

How is this happening? It is happening in the New Testament way. Jesus sent His disciples out to heal the sick, raise the dead, cast out demons and preach the kingdom of God. Check out the history of American missionaries, whom God used in the past to evangelize huge parts of the world. God used the missionaries in spite of the fact that until recently, while they preached the gospel, the message was very rarely accompanied by the signs and wonders that we read about in the New Testament. As a former American missionary, I can personally attest to the fact that at least some of us were taught not to expect to see the sick healed, demons cast out or the dead raised through our ministry. Some of our theologians relegated such things to the lunatic fringe of Christianity.

Nigerian theologians don't seem to have the same intellectual, exegetical, theological or philosophical problems that most

American theologians have had. They simply take Jesus at His word: "He who believes in Me, the works that I do he will do also; and greater works than these he will do, because I go to My Father" (John 14:12). Not only do Nigerian pastors and missionaries believe and practice this, but laypeople do as well. They expect that these signs will follow every believer: "They will cast out demons; they will speak with new tongues; they will take up serpents; and if they drink anything deadly, it will by no means hurt them; they will lay hands on the sick, and they will recover" (Mark 16:17-18).

American Christian leaders who receive up-to-date information such as *The Barna Report* lament the fact that evangelism has all but stalled out in America today. We have much to learn from Nigeria. I know that it will be hard for some readers of this book to believe or assimilate, but the fact of the matter is that there are Nigerians today who literally have lost count of how often God has used them to raise people from the dead. In fact, it will be surprising to some that more of our Nigerian authors do not tell stories of miracles, healings and deliverances. The reason for this is that such occurrences are commonplace in their country. They are as much a part of the normal Christian life as going to church, taking communion, raising children to become believers or treating your neighbor with kindness.

MINISTRY IN THE WORKPLACE

A powerful factor in Nigerian Christian leadership is that few of the major apostles of Nigeria today have been trained for the ministry through the academic process that Americans are accustomed to. The assumption of many American Christians is that in order to be ordained, one must complete a program of studies in a Bible school, a Christian university or a theological seminary.

It is not that Nigerian leaders are uneducated. They are educated, but a large percentage of them have been educated to be workplace professionals. Their teachers were not theologians; rather, they were individuals who understood the world around them and how it operates. Because of this, the connection between the workplace and the church is much stronger in Nigeria than it is here in America. For example, William Kumuyi was a university professor of the philosophy of mathematics before God called him to be a pastor and an apostle.

Among the contributors to this book, Eskor Mfon owns a national advertising agency. Sola Fola-Alade is a medical doctor. Enoch Adeboye was a professor of mathematics. David Oyedepo is a trained architect, as is Paul Adefarasin. Emmanuel Nuhu Kure and Sunday Adelaja both have professional degrees in mass communications and marketing, while Joe Olaiya has a degree in civil engineering. Joseph Thompson, even though he has degrees in theology, originally graduated with a degree in graphic arts with a minor in photography.

Zach Wazara, the author of chapter 8, is the founder and CEO of Econet Wireless Nigeria, one of the two dominant cellular telephone companies in the nation. As you read his chapter, you will agree with me that he is one of the most outstanding role models for a growing number of workplace believers who see their profession as a legitimate call of God, a ministry not only for the transformation of individuals with whom they come into contact but also for the transformation of society as a whole.

READ ON

I believe that we American Christians in all humility must confess that we could use some help from outside if we are to be everything that God wants us to be. It is difficult for us because we have been the greatest missionary-sending nation of all time. Our mentality? America sends missionaries; we do not receive them. It is time, in my opinion, that this thinking change. Let's move into the twenty-first century. Let's be world Christians. Let's be open to what God has to say to us from leaders no matter what their skin color or their nation of origin.

My prayer is that God will use these words of wisdom, birthed from the hearts, lives and experiences of these awesome Nigerian men of God, to impart to us some of what we need to experience the fresh power of God, to lift the Body of Christ in America to a new level, to witness the salvation of multitudes and to see the structures of our society transformed into reflections of the kingdom of God.

If you agree with my prayer, read on.

CHAPTER ONE

RISING FROM THE MEDIOCRE TO THE MIRACULOUS

Joseph Thompson

Originally from Nigeria, Joseph Thompson is the founder of Yeshua Ministries, which focuses on city transformation, church growth and leadership development. Networking, deliverance and spiritual warfare are key components of his ministry.

A gifted teacher of the Bible, Joseph served as associate pastor to Pastor Ted Haggard at New Life Church in Colorado Springs, Colorado, for over four years. In addition to his extensive travel schedule, he currently serves as teaching pastor at New Life.

Joseph's academic background includes a bachelor's degree in graphic arts, a bachelor's degree in Christian ministry and a master's of divinity. He travels across the United States and to many other nations, teaching in local churches, conferences and seminars. His easy and humorous delivery style makes the demand for his ministry continuous. Joseph is the author of a book entitled I'm a Christian, So How Can I Have Demons?

Joseph has lived in the United States for over 12 years. He and Sola, his lovely wife of 15 years, have three children: a son, Demi, and two daughters, Bimi and Temi.

The streets are jammed with people, blurring the lines between pedestrian and vehicular traffic. Some people are dressed in the brightest of colors, in their traditional garb, while others are wearing the more familiar Western business attire. The traffic is bumper-to-bumper and stretches as far as the eye can see. Exhaust fumes pollute the air, adding to the very real discomfort of the humid, 96-degree weather. Horns are blaring angrily as frustrated commuters shout their displeasure at one another. Street hawkers parade their wares along the barely moving lines of traffic, trying to sell everything from cell phones and T-shirts to bootlegged videocassettes of American-made movies that have not yet been officially released in the United States.

Adding to the ever present crescendo of noise and seeming confusion, enterprising young men on mopeds take advantage of the snail-paced traffic. They weave in and out among the cars and offer to transport frustrated commuters who have given up on their taxicabs, usually keeping their promise to get them to their destinations on time. The risk on the moped, however, is being hit by an impatient driver jostling for space to maneuver his or her way out of this virtual parking lot.

In the background are the sounds of laughter and loud conversation as everyone attempts to be heard over the swell of noise. This is Lagos, Nigeria—its myriad exotic smells, its endless cacophony of sounds, its ostentatiously colorful people! This is Africa's most populous nation. In fact, Nigeria boasts the largest concentration of black people on Earth, an estimated 140 million. At the worst of times, it would appear as if they are all out on the streets of Lagos at once!

THE PEARL OF AFRICA

This is what first-time observers see when they visit Nigeria. Underneath all of that activity, however, lies the real Nigeria, the Nigeria that is often referred to as the Pearl of Africa. Nigeria appears, to all intents and purposes, sleepy and unproductive— the one voted most likely to succeed but who ultimately failed.

One writer observed that "Nigeria is an oil-rich Cinderella state that never quite made it to the ball. During the 1970s, when oil prices rocketed, Nigeria looked set to become the shining example of a prosperous and democratic West African republic but perversely managed to snatch defeat from the jaws of victory. It has had the odd moment of oil-induced triumph but its history is littered with tin-pot dictators, massacres, bloody civil wars, human rights abuses, and horrific famines. It is now a country that is saddled with a soaring crime rate, massive unemployment, overpopulation; and it's still recovering from a military government run on bribery and corruption."[1]

If you close your eyes and imagine for just one moment, you could easily believe that I have just described the history of Israel as recorded in the Scriptures. Like the nation of Israel in the days of the kings, Nigeria has had its share of impotent governments and corrupt leaders, but that is Nigeria's history. Its present and future are shaping up to be quite different. A new day has dawned and Nigeria is truly set to become Africa's miracle, fulfilling its destiny as the Pearl of Africa. But before I get ahead of myself, let me give you some insight into Nigeria's beginnings. The details of the following political and economic history primarily come from the study and guide on Nigeria at 1Up Info's website. For further information please consult the guide: www.1upinfo.com/country-guide-study/nigeria/.

THE BIRTH PANGS OF A NATION

Nigeria officially became independent from the colonial rule of the British on October 1, 1960. The nation began as a loose amalgamation of different tribes that were formed into autonomous political regions, but the history of these tribes extends back more than 2,000 years. The country guide at the 1Up Info website records, "The earliest archeological finds were of the Nok, who inhabited the central Jos Plateau between the Niger and the Benue rivers between 300 B.C. and 200 A.D. A number of states or kingdoms with which contemporary ethnic groups can be identified existed before 1500. Of these, the three dominant regional groups were the Hausa in the northern kingdoms of the savanna, the Yoruba in the west, and the Igbo in the south."[2]

The European slave trade in West Africa in the late fifteenth century significantly impacted Nigeria, as Nigeria became a major center for shipping slaves. In 1807 Britain oulawed the slave trade and sent its navy off the coast of West Africa to enforce the ban, ultimately leading to Britain's intervention in Nigeria. During this period, European missionaries began spreading Christianity in southern Nigeria. At the same time, Islam was introduced along the caravan trade routes of northern Nigeria; a holy war waged between 1804 and 1808 was instrumental in the spread of Islam. With Nigeria's rich supplies of palm oil, cocoa and peanuts, commerce with the European powers soon overshadowed the slave trade. Britain established a colony in Lagos in 1861.

Throughout the first half of the twentieth century, Britain controlled Nigeria using local rulers. By the time of World War II, however, Nigerian nationalism was rising. Education and economic development opened the door for an organized labor movement to arise. Various political parties were created during World War II.

Nigeria finally became an independent republic in the early 1960s, but trouble was brewing. Following low voter participation in the 1964-65 elections, widespread violence erupted, which led to the deaths of as many as 2,000 people. After a series of coups and countercoups, Lieutenant Colonel Yakubu Gowon established a military government; and tensions began to increase between the infantry, who were primarily from the North, and the Igbo soldiers, who were from the South. In 1967 the conflict escalated into a civil war, known as the Biafran War. By the end of the war in 1970, about 2 million Nigerians had been killed.[3]

How did this come about?

The Battle for Control

According to research posted at the African Postcolonial Literature in English website, Nigeria began as a republic with four regional governments. This was not a comfortable political situation, especially since the ruling party that dominated the new nation was made up largely of those from only one of the four regions, the North. Explosive ethnic tensions developed between the Igbo from the southeast and the Hausa from the North. Widespread murders on both sides became the order of the day.

In 1966 the four regions unsuccessfully attempted negotiations to return to a republican form of government. The situation deteriorated even more, and in 1967, Lieutenant Colonel Emeka Odumegwu Ojukwu declared the eastern region a sovereign and independent nation, the Republic of Biafra. The federal government declared a state of emergency and divided Nigeria into 12 states. Fighting broke out, and a civil war was on.

The fighting ended in 1970, by which time the federal forces, through starving the Biafran population, had forced them to surrender. Ojukwu fled Nigeria, and a delegation from Biafra formally surrendered on January 15, 1970, ending the short-lived Republic of Biafra.[4]

The Problem of Oil

With the civil war over and the country hoping to rebuild its ailing economy as well as its bruised international image, Nigeria turned to oil as its primary export and foreign exchange earner. Petroleum had been discovered in the late 1960s in commercial quantities, and in 1971, Nigeria became a member of the Organization of Petroleum Exporting Countries (OPEC).[5]

Rather than strengthen the Nigerian economy, however, the discovery of oil created unforeseen problems. Foreign investors reaped most of the profits, while the local indigenous people in the oil-producing regions gained little or nothing. Policymakers demonstrated their deplorable lack of foresight by granting "Udoji awards," bonuses for every government worker as a result of increased oil revenue. Meanwhile, they tended to neglect all other national resources that had previously undergirded the nation's economy. Nigeria was experiencing a classic case of the rich getting richer and the poor getting poorer.

In addition, the economy suffered dearly from a three-year drought in the early 1970s, forcing huge numbers of farm workers to relocate in the cities.

After another series of military coups, in 1976 Lieutenant General Olusegun Obasanjo came to power; and in 1979 a new constitution, calling for democratic elections, was drafted. Obasanjo focused on preparing Nigeria for the upcoming democracy.

A combination of the weak political structure, the problems associated with the discovery of oil and fraud in the 1983 elections caused the army to step in once again. Major General Muhammed Buhari, who determined to end widespread corruption, became head of state. However, he was deposed by the Armed Forces Ruling Council, which purported to prepare Nigeria for a return to civilian rule. This took the form of economic restructuring. A national economic emergency was declared in 1986, and as a result, Nigeria received aid from the World Bank.[6]

The Nigerian Brain Drain

Along with all of these economic, tribal and political tensions were frightening increases in corruption, armed robbery and drug dealing, for which Nigerians were fast developing international notoriety. Student riots became more frequent and more violent, and outspoken dissenters would suddenly either disappear or end up in prison.

Universities would be shut down for months on end as a result of student unrest, and pretty soon both students and professors began to seek opportunities outside the country. These educational crises, coupled with massive inflation that raised the cost of living to unbearable standards, preceded what has come to be known as the Brain Drain. Many of Nigeria's best qualified academicians began relocating to other countries where they and their families could enjoy a higher standard of living. As a result, the government embarked on a huge campaign to encourage the educated Nigerian elite to stay in the country and help rebuild the crumbled economy. A clarion call for patriotism was heard across various media.

During this period, Nigerian morale reached an all-time low. Inflation, poverty and widespread corruption became the order of the day. What was the government's response to the cry of the people against the tyranny of injustice? "We cannot afford to complain as long as we haven't resorted to eating out of trash cans." This represented a sad departure from the Nigeria of old, for which the standing joke was, "Money isn't our problem in Nigeria; it's how to spend it that is the problem!"

AN OPEN DOOR TO THE DEMONIC

The year was 1977 and the Lagos traffic stretched the length of Western Avenue all the way to Iganmu. Eko Bridge was bumper-to-bumper in both directions and the pedestrian traffic was thick. An atmosphere of festivity filled the air as flags from every African nation adorned the streetlights running the length of Eko Bridge. All the traffic seemed to converge at one spot, the National Arts Theater. This superb edifice, a monument to Nigeria's oil wealth, stood proudly isolated from all other structures. Costing millions of American dollars to build and designed to look like a military general's cap, it was an ingenious feat of architecture built on swampland, which also cost millions of dollars to dredge. The occasion for all the festivity was FESTAC 77, the second World Black and African Festival of Arts and Culture. This event was designed to be a showcase of African cultural identity. It issued "a clarion call for all Africans throughout diasporas, to come home to invoke and celebrate the Motherland." It was billed as a "historic Gathering of Tribes."[7]

Listen to what Joseph Okpaku says in volume 8 of *The Arts and Civilization of Black and African Peoples*:

When a people, indeed an entire race, decide to formally define their place in history and to dramatize that demarcation by asserting their unquestionably important position and role as a primary cornerstone of mankind, such an event is significant. When that race is Africa with its colossal cultural and intellectual heritage, that occasion promises overwhelming inspiration.[8]

The overarching idea behind FESTAC 77 was the rediscovery of the cultural and spiritual ties which bind together all black and African people the world over. Rediscovering African traditional currents of thought and arts was paramount. Therein lay the root of Nigeria's problems. There is where the dark doors began to open.

The colorful display of culture and the demonstration of Africa's rich and varied heritage were not all that was celebrated during FESTAC 77. Africa has always been a continent with a strong animistic heritage. The celebration and worship of multiple gods in the form of graven images cannot be divorced from African arts and culture. Unwittingly, as we celebrated the reuniting of our cultural and artistic heritage, we were also laying out a welcome mat for all of the ominous spiritual forces embedded in the various African cultures. The celebration of an animistic heritage and consequently of idols, along with their accompanying demons, carries with it grave consequences. The Bible has made it abundantly clear that God is displeased with the worship of any other god besides Him:

> However, if you do not obey the LORD your God and do not carefully follow all his commands and decrees I am giving you today, all these curses will come upon you and overtake you. The LORD will send on you curses, confusion and rebuke in everything you put your hand

to, until you are destroyed and come to sudden ruin because of the evil you have done in forsaking him (Deut. 28:15,20, *NIV*).

The manifest fruit of this curse became evident in Nigeria post-FESTAC 77. Inflation hit an all-time high, and people literally began to scrounge and forage for food in trash cans. The self-fulfilling prophecy was being manifest before our very

While it seemed like the demonic forces had taken over, another force was at work: the Spirit of God.

eyes. Unemployment, increasing widespread corruption, bribery and violence became the order of the day. People began to turn overtly to witchdoctors and fortune-tellers for answers to their problems. This introduced a spate of kidnappings and occult ritual killings that spread fear among the population. People became less and less inclined to leave their homes after dark, and many parts of the country ceased to have any kind of active nightlife. This only got worse through the civilian-ruled era of the late 1970s and early 1980s. It began to look like our beloved country was on the very brink of destruction and anarchy.

While it seemed like the demonic forces had taken over, another force was at work: the Spirit of God. He was calling His Church to rise up and pray, to become active in society and to see His presence transform it.

The Church at War

The intensity of prayer reached fever pitch as the crowd avidly responded to the prayer leader. There was a heightened sense of anticipation among the people as some paced back and forth in the sanctuary, while others kneeled and still others sat silently, rocking back and forth as if keeping time with the soft worship music playing in the background. Many lay sprawled flat on their faces as they cried out to God for His intervention in the affairs of their nation in order to prevent it from sliding into complete genocide. Most of these zealously patriotic Nigerians had been fasting for a week or more leading up to this final, culminating annual event.

It was the first of October, 1987, the anniversary of Nigeria's independence day celebration. While many were at the race course taking in all the festivities displaying Nigeria's rich and diverse heritage, these select few Christians were groaning in travail for the very soul of the nation. As the prayers became more specific, people from different tribes were called out to pray and repent on behalf of their people, for tribalism as well as for various other sins that had become associated with their people group. Mass repentance was done on behalf of one tribe toward another, and intercession was made on behalf of governmental leaders who had turned away from God and from their commitment to serve the people. The prayer meeting lasted almost six hours, into the early evening, and when it was over, there was the unspoken promise that the believers would meet at the same time, in the same place, the following year, until there is an evident transformation and a full return to God in the nation.

This was an annual prayer event in which I was privileged to participate. Many years back, as the debilitating attrition of inflation and corruption began to infect every stratum of Nigerian society, people began their search for something better.

At this juncture, a major move of God began to sweep across our university campuses and other institutions of higher learning. For the first time, the educated elite began to consider Christianity as a viable answer to the problems we were facing as a nation. Numerous campus fellowships sprang up, and it was no longer considered uncool to be a Christian. Christ Chapel was one of the first charismatic-style churches catering to the needs of this new breed of Nigerian Christians. Thousands began flocking to this church and to similar ones to find spiritual fulfillment.

The New Breed of Christian Leaders

It was in the midst of all this that the annual prayer gathering developed. Led by a number of professionals who were lawyers, engineers, doctors, architects and the like, it quickly became a leading voice for the educated Christians who were seeking to make a difference in the nation through prayer. Men such as Emeka Nwakpa, Tunde Ogunnaike, Steve Okitika, Kole Akinboboye and Ntiense Inyang were the driving forces behind this powerful prayer movement. They were all leaders in an organization called Christian Students Social Movement, and they were responsible in large part for the spread of other prayer initiatives around the country. The annual prayer gathering that I chose to attend was held at a Presbyterian church in Yaba, Lagos.

Inevitably, as a result of this and numerous other prayer movements like it, God began to move. The influence and impact of Christianity began to spread across the nation at various levels of the culture.

I would be remiss, however, if I left you thinking that only the people I have mentioned spearheaded this revival movement. Men like William Kumuyi, who while teaching the philosophy of mathematics at the University of Lagos (UNILAG) had begun a

Monday night fellowship in his home, mostly catering to students from UNILAG as well as the nearby Yaba College of Technology, were instrumental. Leaders like Tunde Ogunnaike, who was a student at UNILAG at the time, had been influenced by Kumuyi's fellowship. Dr. Enoch A. Adeboye, at the time a professor of mathematics at UNILAG, was also a significant leader in the wave of revival that swept across the nation. Indeed, most of the contributors to this book were all significant players in the spread and influence of charismatic Christianity across Nigeria.

A Great Awakening

The melody fills the air with a heavenly sound as the crowd of thousands sing out the words to the song with gusto. The look on their faces is one of rapturous delight, and to an outsider, they appear oblivious to anything else going on around them. Neither the perspiration dripping off their faces due to the 99-degree weather nor the cramped quarters serves to deter them from the singular purpose of worship. The crowd is a mixture of young college students, apparently successful professionals and a more sedate looking middle-aged group of obviously financially well-off people. Their clothing is more befitting of a group of people at an exclusive banquet rather than the regular Sunday morning service of the House of Faith Church. And this scene is duplicated in myriad churches across the nation every Sunday. Literally millions of hope-filled Christians throng their local assemblies, secure in the knowledge that God is not finished with Nigeria. Pleas and prayers fill the heavens as voices from every tribe mingle together in an outpouring of devotion to Jesus Christ. The only notable difference from one congregation to the next is the name of the local assembly and the obvious differences in social and educational status.

The Impact of Christianity

"Nigeria we hail thee" has once again become an appropriate recognition for our reemerging great nation. Taken from the opening stanza of our former national anthem, the line "Nigeria we hail thee" has never rung so true. We hail thee for the resilience shown through the years of unrestrained plunder. We hail thee for never giving up when all seemed lost. But most important, we hail thee because of the faith and commitment you have shown as a people to the unfailing truth of God's Word.

Nigeria is back on track! Nigeria is a nation that is festooned with the beauty of Christianity.

Nigeria is back on track! Nigeria is a nation that is festooned with the beauty of Christianity. It is safe to say that the Church and its effectual prayers have kept Nigeria from complete anarchy and genocide. The impact of Christianity on its hitherto beleaguered society is evident wherever you go. If you look a little deeper, listen a little more closely, you will see and hear the myriad changes that are subtly transforming Nigeria into a nation that truly fears the Lord.

The Impact on Nigerian Society

Today, Nigeria is a nation that boasts a president who is a professed Christian. Significant numbers of leaders in politics and industry are coming to the awareness that Jesus is Lord and

Savior. Christianity is touted from every other automobile in the form of bumper stickers and from slogans painted on trucks. There is a new sense of purpose and direction as churches are recognizing that ministry must be to the total person: spirit, soul and body. For the first time since the colonization of Nigeria and the subsequent founding of schools and hospitals by missionaries, the Church is once again involved in establishing schools with high ethical and moral standards, schools that teach only the truths about creation and God. Many churches in Nigeria have established hospitals, banks, soup kitchens and other such institutions designed to meet the social needs of the day. The miraculous power of God is evident in the Church in Nigeria, but just as evident is His love for Nigeria and its people. There is such a radical move of God on university and college campuses in Nigeria that thousands of students are turning to the Lord on a daily basis.

The Impact on Nigerian Muslims

The amazing growth of the Church in Nigeria is spawning a rather intriguing phenomenon. Muslims, who traditionally meet on Friday afternoon for their large prayer meetings, have resorted to imitating Christian all-night prayer vigils as well as Sunday services in an effort to stem the tide of young people converting from Islam to Christianity. They are establishing prayer camps just like the ones they see in the Christian Church, in the hope that they will discover some formula to stem the dramatic surge of Christianity in Nigeria.

The Impact on Other Nations

This powerful move of God is not limited to Nigerians in Nigeria alone. As you will read in chapter 2, some of the largest churches around the world were planted by Nigerians. Unarguably,

Nigerians pastor the largest churches found in Europe, in the United Kingdom, in Ghana, in Jamaica and in Italy, as well as in many other countries. In the United States alone, the Redeemed Christian Church of God has over 20 branch churches, and the average attendance at most of them exceeds 500. Many of these churches do not cater exclusively to Nigerians but have as diverse a membership as can be imagined. In Denver, Colorado, my good friend, Ade Ajala, is senior pastor of Hands On Christian Church, which has 17 different nations represented in its membership. Most of the members are new converts, and they are aggressively reaching out to other foreign nationals resident in their community. For example, they have recently had to add a Spanish service in order to meet the needs of the many Spanish-speaking people who have come to Christ and joined their church.

A DIVINE VISITATION

What could be responsible for this sudden and powerful move of God both in Nigeria and among Nigerians living outside of their nation? Well, I can tell you what is not responsible, and that is a bottled formula. There is not some special dispensation of revelation that came upon the Nigerian Church, causing its suddenly to prosper. No. This is simply a sovereign move of God in response to the fervent prayers of a spiritually, physically and emotionally tortured nation. Hear what the prophet Isaiah had to say about the fervent prayers (travail) of a nation:

> Who hath heard such a thing? who hath seen such things? Shall the earth be made to bring forth in one day? *or shall a nation be born at once? for as soon as Zion travailed, she brought forth her children* (Isa. 66:8, *KJV*, emphasis added).

What an honor! What a privilege! We are witnessing a true miracle of biblical proportions right before our eyes: the rebirth of a nation. Nigeria is being stretched and squeezed, forged in the fires of God's plans and purposes, and slowly but surely is emerging as a pearl of inestimable value, a priceless jewel of great worth. Or in the inimitable words of the apostle Paul, an epistle to be read by all (see 1 Thess. 5:27).

STEWARDSHIP OF THE REVIVAL

The greatest injustice we Nigerian Christian leaders could do to the next generation of leaders is to fail to leave a lasting legacy of the divine visitation that our nation is currently experiencing. I am reminded of a story I read about a woodworker in Germany named Stefan. Stefan produces wood for various purposes. He does this by harvesting trees that were planted by his great-grandfather, whom he never knew. This line of work has been in Stefan's family for 400 years. Stefan knows that if this family legacy is to continue, he must plant trees that he will never harvest. His grandchildren or great-grandchildren will probably harvest them. Stefan is reliant on the past but also responsible for the future.[9]

If we leaders are to bequeath a godly legacy to our great nation, then we must steward the revival that God is granting today so that it produces true and permanent reformation. We must recognize that the fruit we are now harvesting has come from seeds sown with the blood of many missionaries who invested their lives in our people while we were predominantly animistic. It is therefore incumbent on us, like Stefan, to plant "trees" for future generations to harvest.

I am well aware that this is easier said than done. Because Nigeria is such a tribally influenced nation, it is sometimes harder for us to free ourselves from that paradigm and be willing to take people from different tribes under our tutelage for the purpose of investing in the future. We must begin to recognize that the anointing is not necessarily transferred down a bloodline in a family or, for that matter, through ethnic or tribal lines, but it is distributed according to the sovereign will of the Holy Spirit. When we recognize this, we will begin to realize that experiencing the visitation of God upon our nation is not a tribal or family heritage but a national treasure to be preserved and stewarded for the next generation.

Many foreign observers of the move of God in Nigeria have remarked that the Church may be a mile wide but only an inch deep. They draw this conclusion based on the huge number of churches they see spread across the country, prospering right beside teeming masses of poverty, corruption and illiteracy. My response to this is simply to state that it is unfair to expect an immediately evident and dramatic change in a nation that has been so plundered. Nigeria has emerged from its turmoil landing on its feet, primarily because of the grace of God in response to the cry of the Church.

Slowly but surely, change is becoming evident to all through the work of the Church. For example, as you will read in more detail in chapter 11, the church City of David is feeding no fewer than 30,000 people every Sunday. Bishop David Oyedepo's Canaan Land provides subsidized bus transportation in a fleet of over 200 buses and vans that operate at the church's expense. Many Nigerian churches are building hospitals, schools and banks that provide affordable and good health care, decent academic training and loans to help Christian entrepreneurs who otherwise would be unable to establish businesses. These, in turn, provide employment. These, I believe, are several ways that we can effectively steward this move of God, which we are privileged to be a part of, so that future generations will reap the legacy we leave them.

CHAPTER TWO

GO TO A LAND THAT I WILL SHOW YOU!

Sunday Adelaja

Sunday Adelaja is a young, visionary, Nigerian-born leader with an apostolic gift for the twenty-first century. Now in his mid 30s, Pastor Sunday has already proven himself to be one of the world's most dynamic communicators and church planters.

He pastors one of the largest churches in Europe, with a congregation of over 20,000 members. Remarkably, he does this in Ukraine. His

*church, Embassy of God, which is only eight years old, has already plant-
ed over 200 churches in other countries such as the United Arab Emirates,
the United States, the Netherlands, Russia and many others.*

*Adelaja is recognized as one of the most gifted teachers of the Word
of God in our time, with an unusual operation of the gifts of the Spirit,
especially the word of knowledge. His teaching and use of these gifts have
contributed in no small measure to the rapid growth of his congregation.
A proven leader, Sunday is well known for his strategy of discipling
groups of 12 leaders, whom he subsequently sends out to plant new
churches.*

*Sunday is happily married to Bose, "Princess," and they are blessed
with three children, Perez, Zoe and Pearl.*

The world news on the Nigerian television channel 10 had just
finished. The young 19-year-old viewer was contemplating
whether he should keep watching to see what the next program
might be or to look for something better to do. The seemingly
insignificant decision to keep watching ended up changing the
whole life of that teenager, who, as you may have guessed, was
me. The next program was a stadium crusade featuring Pastor
William Kumuyi. Through his anointed preaching, I clearly
understood the gospel for the first time, and immediately I
committed my life to the Lord. Little could I have imagined that
my experience back in 1986 would eventually affect a whole
nation on the other side of the world!

But God knew!

DESTINATION: RUSSIA

Like many young Nigerians finishing high school, I began search-
ing newspaper advertisements for a government scholarship to

study in one of the leading Nigerian universities. The tuition and the cost of living in a university was something my family could no longer afford.

I say "no longer" because the Adelaja family at one time was prosperous, one of the most highly respected families in our part of Nigeria. Not only did we easily send family members to study at a university, but we also provided scholarships for less fortunate families in our region. Then tragedy struck! The three brothers who were the pillars of my extended family all died unexpected, violent deaths within just a few months of each other. Without the pillars, the family crumbled and was left destitute.

Just as God called Paul on the Damascus road, so He was calling me.

That is why I became one of the first of the prominent Adelajas to find himself "begging" for a scholarship. My search narrowed down to two options: Columbia State University in the United States or Byelarussian State University in the former Soviet Union.

The advantage I had is that I knew God, and I could pray and ask Him for advice. He directed me to go to Russia in a way reminiscent of the call He gave to Abraham: "Get out of your country, from your family and from your father's house, to a land that I will show you" (Gen. 12:1). Even though I was a new believer, I had the faith to accept this as God's sovereign assignment for my future destiny. Later I realized that this was actually my missionary call; just as God called Paul on the Damascus road, so He was calling me. However, He did not reveal it to me then, because I would have had no way of even understanding what a missionary call might possibly have been.

A Not-So-Smooth Beginning

After two weeks in Russia, I wanted to go home. I found myself in a dingy hotel room. The tall, drab apartment buildings, the gray weather, the look of hopelessness on the faces of the people and the spiritually dry Sunday mornings with no church or fellowship with other believers all fed my growing disillusion. My naïve image of Russia's being a super economic power just like America came crashing down in a matter of days. Just as I was contemplating returning to Africa, I heard God whisper in my heart, "I directed you here and I have a purpose for bringing you to this place."

These words convinced me to push forward. I settled into my studies at Byelarussian State University, majoring in journalism. I immediately started a search for what I had heard called the underground church. A few days later, I came across a couple of Christian foreign students who met secretly on the university campus. I joined them, and then the struggle to escape the all-penetrating eyes of the KGB began.

My Clash with the Law

The only encounter I ended up having with the law occurred because I was becoming too bold in displaying my faith. My offense was having hung a picture of the Crucifixion over my bed. It was a cold afternoon, after the day's classes, when loud banging at my door sounded the warning. Four men from the Youth Communist Party as well as my professors came in. They demanded that I remove the picture of Jesus or be dismissed from the university, since Soviet law prohibits religious propaganda. My flesh wanted to enter into a dispute to defend my Lord, but the soft, sweet voice of the Holy Spirit spoke to my heart again, "Let them remove it; only don't allow them to

> *Survival during Communism's dictatorship demanded much wisdom, silent worship and many narrow escapes by the power of the Holy Spirit—lessons never to be forgotten!*

remove Him from your heart." After I removed the picture from the wall, the conflict with the government died out as simply as it had begun.

Not all of my classmates and colleagues were as fortunate as I, however. As time went by, some were dismissed from the university, while others ended up in psychiatric confinement before being sent out of the country. Survival during Communism's dictatorship demanded much wisdom, silent worship and many narrow escapes by the power of the Holy Spirit—lessons never to be forgotten! During the six-year journey to my master's in journalism, there were many instances when I thought I would either go crazy or be deported once and for all. But the mercy and goodness of the Lord were with me.

Christian Casualties

As difficult as it was to survive the presence and persecution of Communism, there were many more Christian casualties as a result of other factors. Sadly, sex, money and carefree living stole the faith of many of the Christians who came into the former Soviet Union. In a society in which God had been officially declared nonexistent, sin and immorality became the order of the day. Since there was no God, there could be no sin.

This deception actually took the life of my close friend Brother Tom. We had entered the country together as professing Christians. We prayed together and lived in the same dormitory until, after language school, Tom was transferred to Kiev to continue his studies. The next time I heard about Tom, he had become a womanizer and an alcoholic—another lesson for me. The only strategy for survival in such spiritually challenging circumstances is the fear of God.

> The fear of the LORD is to hate evil; pride and arrogance and the evil way and the perverse mouth I hate (Prov. 8:13).

The fear of the Lord kept me focused till the year 1990, when the God-ordained reformations of Mikhail Gorbachev began to take effect. For the first time, we were able to meet with Russian believers. That turned out to be the beginning of my full-time ministry. However, the call of God on my life had occurred some time before that.

MY MISSIONARY CALL

In one of the underground meetings, the leader of the group of foreigners, while encouraging us to remain steadfast in the Lord, asked us to seek the face of the Lord as to why He might have brought us to Russia in the first place. I heartily accepted the challenge. I prayed morning and night for two weeks, asking God to show me why He had brought me to Russia. At the end of the second week, something extraordinary began to happen to me. For three consecutive nights I had a dream of God showing His plans and future for me. My diary records:

October 31, 1986
Today is the third day I'm receiving such a visitation from the Lord. Today also, I had a dream in which I saw myself before a large crowd of thousands of people. I saw myself on the stage ministering beside one of the leading world ministers. He seemed to step aside and hand the microphone to me, then I continued to minister to the people. Immediately, after waking up baffled, I opened my Bible spontaneously to Isaiah 61, a passage I had never noticed before:

> The spirit of the Lord GOD is upon me; because the LORD hath anointed me to preach good tidings unto the meek; he hath sent me to bind up the brokenhearted, to proclaim liberty to the captives, and the opening of the prison to them that are bound; to proclaim the acceptable year of the LORD, and the day of vengeance of our God; to comfort all that mourn; to appoint unto them that mourn in Zion, to give unto them beauty for ashes, the oil of joy for mourning, the garment of praise for the spirit of heaviness; that they might be called trees of righteousness, the planting of the LORD, that he might be glorified. And they shall build the old wastes, they shall raise up the former desolations, and they shall repair the waste cities, the desolations of many generations. And strangers shall stand and feed your flocks, and the sons of the alien

shall be your plowmen and your vinedressers
(Isa. 61:1-5, *KJV*).

After receiving this, as well as other Scriptures, I went to Brother
Paul Dahunsi, the leader of our group. Later that day, in my
diary I wrote:

> Today, November 1, 1986, Brother Paul told me God had
> given him a message for a member of the fellowship last
> night. As soon as I finished narrating my story to him,
> he said the message was for me. "God cannot afford to
> give precious materials to cowards or careless children.
> God needs people who will not toy with firsthand infor-
> mation—people who will not give what is meant for the
> children to the dogs. You must be trustworthy, careful,
> ready, serious and observant before things can be
> entrusted to your hands. Be prepared!" This was a con-
> firmation of my call.

WILDERNESS TRAINING

Though I was finishing my studies in journalism, I knew by
then that I would not be going into professional practice. The
revelation that I was going into full-time ministry was burning
in my heart. I strongly and urgently felt I needed ministry
preparation, so I got in touch with a famous charismatic Bible
institute in America. I was accepted, but as I prayed about this,
God gave me an unexpected answer. He clearly said, "I have different ways of preparing my generals. One way is by linking
them with existing leaders in the Body of Christ. Another way is
through Bible school. A third means of preparation is raising
up the leaders in the context of a strong local church. However,
when I want to do something truly extraordinary, I take My
generals to the wilderness. Russia is your wilderness. It is the

Bible school I have prepared especially for you." That revelation from God gave me much understanding about all I had been going through under Communism. I was in Bible school in the wilderness!

Once we began enjoying President Gorbachev's reforms, I started traveling all over the countries of the former Soviet Union, planting churches, preaching and teaching. This continued until some of my friends and I were rounded up in one city of Belarus by the KGB—I had just finished my master's program in journalism. The Belarus government and the KGB ordered me to leave the country. I managed to stay in the country and fight the deportation until the Lord moved me to Kiev, Ukraine.

My Call to Ukraine

It was years later when I finally understood that I was actually resisting God's will by praying against leaving Belarus. Kiev was where God had wanted me all along. Thank God He didn't answer my prayer to remain in Belarus! For me to get into Ukraine, God had to perform a series of miracles, since I had never even considered Ukraine as an option. If I left Belarus, I naturally thought that I would go back to Nigeria. But through amazing circumstances, God put me in Kiev.

During my period of struggling to stay in Belarus, I received a call from some of my African friends in Ukraine. Due to their semester and school engagements, they couldn't accept an invitation to translate for Pastor Jeff Davis of Tulsa, Oklahoma, who was going to give a series of teachings all over Ukraine. They wanted me to step in for them. Only God knew how much I resisted that assignment—for one thing, I did not have the money to buy a ticket to Kiev—but God enabled me to beat the odds by sovereignly guiding my footsteps. So I served as Jeff Davis's interpreter.

It was not more than a few weeks after I had returned to Belarus that I received a call from Jeff Davis. He had just signed a contract with an independent, commercial television station in Kiev, and he needed a person who could represent his interests. That person had to be, first, a Christian and, second, a professional journalist. The only person he knew with such qualifications was me, he said. This happened at the exact time I was praying about where to move after leaving Belarus. A few months later, my Ukrainian visa, an apartment, a company car and a director's chair were awaiting me in Kiev, Ukraine!

FROM TELEVISION TO PASTORING

As I worked at the channel 7 television station in Kiev, the general director, Slava Bun, discovered how different I was—I did not smoke, drink or run around with girls. My explanation for not doing these things was that I felt called to share the gospel with him and my other coworkers. Slava became so curious that he asked me to create a program based on Christian values. That is how God opened up the opportunity for me to minister for a year in a weekly hour-long program—and all for free!

By the end of 1993, I could no longer resist the urge of the Spirit to plant a church in Kiev. In November, at my apartment I started a Bible study program that attracted about seven people. I trained them three times a week, with a three-hour lesson each time, for three months. By February 1994, we had grown to about 49 people. At that time the new church went public under the name Word of Faith Bible Church, which in 2002 became Embassy of the Blessed Kingdom of God for All Nations.

As I kept asking God to show me His purposes for the church, He told me first that it was to be a megachurch to win and minister to thousands of people from the Kiev area. And just as important, the second purpose for the church would be to send missionaries into the world, especially into China and the Arab countries. Just as the world used to know the former Soviet Union as an exporter of weapons of mass destruction, so now God wanted these nations to be exporters of life through the gospel of the kingdom of God. Today I stand amazed at how the Lord has helped us through the years to be faithful to this call.

A CHURCH TO KEEP

When I had first arrived in Ukraine, I had determined not to start another church because I couldn't understand why God had me leave Minsk, Belarus, and the new church I had started there. All of my plans had been in place, and I knew God had told me to plant the church there; but then suddenly I was gone. Although I had planted several other churches in Belarus and then had turned them over to nationals, this time I felt that I should pastor the new church. I felt that giving up the leadership of the church in Minsk was like a breast-feeding mother giving up her suckling infant.

When I asked the Lord why He didn't allow me to pastor those churches, His answer was unforgettable: He had instructed me to give them up in their infancy because He never wanted my heart to be embedded in them. That is to say, He didn't ever want me to see a church as my own corporation with myself as the head, owner and operator. It was then that God specifically taught me never to build a denomination. Neither did He ever want me to build a pyramid or hierarchy answerable to me. Instead, I was always to see myself as the manager, who is entrusted only with the temporary caretaking of God's church. That meant that at any time, the true owner of the church could order me either to leave that position or to give over the church to someone else as He instructed me. God knew that I needed to learn to detach myself from the churches I planted in Belarus, despite the fact that they were only in the birthing stage. I learned that the church must never be my own thing! Even though the Lord may use me to start a church or ministry, I must not see myself as the president for life or the supreme authority. I am

> *I learned that even though the Lord may use me to start a church or ministry, I must not see myself as the president for life or the supreme authority.*

there only as long as He allows me to be, and I should always be ready to relinquish it if need be, maybe for another mission field or another country.

Once that lesson was firmly established in my heart and in my mind, God released me to plant a new church in Kiev. This time He directed me to pastor it, not to turn it over in its infancy to the charge of another.

Today, by the grace of God, our church in Kiev is well over 20,000 people strong. But because of the lesson the Lord taught me—never to attach my heart to the work but only to Him—I am ever ready by the grace of God to hand over the ministry to someone else at anytime, as the Lord instructs. This freedom is probably one of my greatest assets in ministry today. Nor am I afraid to release pastors, ministers, evangelists and apostles from our ministry to independently start a fresh work.

We now have 20 branches from our church in Kiev; they all have their own church name, structure, financial policies and accountability. This is also the case with over 300 more daughter churches. All are free to relate to me as the senior pastor, or apostolic covering, which they gladly do. Thanks to this policy, we have never experienced a split or break away from our church. All of our churches know that they have already been released to become an independent work if they so wish. My obligation is to help them get their feet on the ground, help them financially for a year, train them spiritually and release them to accomplish God's will through them. From then on, they have the choice whether or not to remain affiliated.

My relationships are so strong with the ministers I mentor that I have decided never to build an organization. I want to invest my life in building leaders. My dream is not to leave behind an organization when I die, but rather it is to leave a legacy of men and women who have a vision to spread the good news of the Kingdom worldwide. I think this focus is one of the reasons the Lord has chosen to bless our work, giving us over 300 churches in only eight years.

I do not doubt that in the years to come we will see an even greater acceleration of growth, because it is only now that most of our new believers are attaining maturity. There is nothing that can stop the potential of a church that is totally released to do for God anything that the Lord calls it to do. There is tremendous freedom when people know that they are not building an empire for the person at the top. When church members know that they are not being used by their leaders, but rather that their leaders are there to serve them and add value through them, nothing can stop them.

The High Price of Growth

The growth that we have experienced didn't come without a price, however. Over the first three years we moved to six different locations in the city, each time losing a number of people in the process. The church was miraculously registered with the government—despite the vows of some government officials never to allow that to happen. The story we will never forget, however, is the conspiracy, which began after our third-year anniversary, to close down our church and have me deported from Ukraine.

False Accusations

During one of our conferences, we were worshiping and celebrating the greatness of God. The halls were fully packed. The parking lot was too small. People were standing everywhere, including outside the building. As we were rejoicing inside, the police force was mobilizing to put an end, once and for all, to this "uncontrollable sect." On the last day of the conference, our building was surrounded by the police. Fortunately for me, I was not arrested that day, but I was summoned to the police station the following morning. That was the beginning of a horrible chain of events that would last for two full years. All imaginable and unimaginable excuses were found as the basis for deporting me from the country and closing our church.

For example, one of the problems was caused by worldly parents who didn't want their children to attend our church. They claimed that we were desocializing their children, because several children had stopped watching television, others had stopped dating, while some others had begun to criticize the ungodly behavior of their peers and family members. Consequently, I was accused of brainwashing the youth. It should be noted that the youngest of these "youths" was 20 years of age. As this case became public, it precipitated so many arguments in the media that the government set up a committee of psychologists and psychiatrists to investigate the matter and to submit a report on our church and the people who attended it. To the glory of the Lord, the commission came to the conclusion that nothing abnormal could be noted in the health or psyche of our church members.

Soon after the conclusion of that investigation, the secret and intelligence services began another investigation into the charges that I was planning to overthrow the government and take leadership of the country. My passport was seized, my visa was canceled, and a deportation letter was issued by the Ukrainian attorney general. Other charges included dealing drugs, being a Nigerian, making illicit business transactions, embezzling the church's money and so on.

The church was desperate for God to stop this unfair assault on us. My deportation at that stage of the church's development could have dealt a deadly blow since we were only three years old. Moreover, 90 percent of the church consisted of new believers. We appealed to the Body of Christ all over the world to pray for us, and huge numbers fervently did so. Our church declared a 40-day fast. I had always believed and taught that if there is a long-lasting problem, it is only because we have not prayed or we have not prayed enough. On the basis of that belief, I locked myself up for days, praying as much as 16 to 18 hours nonstop each day and fasting. After all, I reasoned, this nonsense had been going on for months and instead of the problems disappearing, they seemed to be getting worse!

A Midcourse Correction

Suddenly I realized that God wanted to correct something. God showed me that the mere ritual of prayer and fasting was not enough. Along with that, I had to learn to say, "God, please don't stop this problem until I've learned all the lessons You want to teach me through this trial." It began to dawn on me that my maturity in faith would not be possible until I passed through the crucible of trials, persecutions and even suffering.

Though he was a Son, yet He learned obedience by the things which He suffered (Heb. 5:8).

The lesson was well understood. When I face a situation and I pray and bind and resist the enemy, and yet nothing changes, I may need to look inside myself for the answer. Maybe God was allowing these hardships. In my situation, the horrible newspaper articles continued to be written on a daily basis, but I stopped reading them and stopped being concerned about them and, for that matter, about my visa and passport. I left myself in His hands!

The Turnaround

Then the signs of a turnaround appeared. Members of parliament started joining the church after some major miracles of God occurred in their lives and in the lives of their family members. As a result, they started lobbying for me in parliament, where they were able to get 50 parliamentarians to sign in my defense. This momentarily put a hold on the decision of the attorney general. The only thing that could settle the dispute between the executive arm of the government and the parliament was the court. There were 22 lawsuits against the church involving different government agencies, media, government officials and so on. At the end of 2000, my ordeal, which had begun in February 1997, ended with the courts decreeing that I should not only be acquitted of the charges but that I also should be issued a resident permit to enable me to lead a constructive and needed institution in the land.

As the years of persecution by the government, press, media and traditional Orthodox Church continued, I continued to tell God that if there were only 20 members left in the church, I would count it worthwhile to keep pursuing my missionary activities in Ukraine. I sincerely felt that 20 would be a good number, given all the social, mental and governmental pressures to which church members had been subjected. But contrary to my expectations, by the time the persecution ended we had grown from 3,000 to 8,000 members. Two years later, the church had 20,000 members with over 300 other churches worldwide.

THE BIG PICTURE

We have come a long way in the journey during the first eight years of Embassy of the Blessed Kingdom of God for All Nations. Here are some statistics as of 2002 that demonstrate how the grace of God has blessed our church:

- Over 20 services are held every Sunday in various auditoriums in Kiev.
- There are 48 daughter churches functioning in the Kiev region—20 in the city of Kiev and 28 in outlying districts.
- There are over 100 daughter churches in the cities and villages of Ukraine.
- There are over 200 daughter churches in the countries of the former Soviet Union, the United States, Germany, the United Arab Emirates, Israel and the Netherlands.
- More than 1 million people have accepted Jesus Christ as their Lord and Savior through our ministry.
- There are over 2,500 home groups with over 3,000 leaders of home groups and outreaches.
- More than 50 percent of the members are actively involved in volunteer ministries.
- Over 300 ministries and outreaches function in the church.
- More than 2,000 people have been set free from drug and alcohol addiction in the church's rehabilitation center.
- The church is attended by a wide spectrum of the society: from former addicts to pop stars, senators, major business tycoons and so on.

- In the church's soup kitchen, 2,000 people are fed daily.
- The church ministers to hundreds of abandoned street kids.
- The church has made printed and recorded resources available, and I personally have authored over 30 books and have recorded over 1,000 sermons.
- The church's Christian television and radio programs reach approximately 8 million people weekly.
- Tens of thousands of people from different cities and countries gather for the anniversary of the church and the various conferences that are conducted regularly.
- With over 20,000 members in Kiev, Embassy of the Blessed Kingdom of God for All Nations is widely regarded as both the largest evangelical and the largest charismatic church in Europe.

My goal in ministry is to raise up leaders and teach them what the Lord has taught me. To this end, I have raised a team of 12 pastors and leaders, whom I train as apostles and with whom I spend up to 10 hours weekly. My first apostolic team has already been sent out by God's direction to plant new churches in other parts of the world. I continue to mentor and train a second apostolic team.

PRINCIPLES FOR GROWTH

I am still a young man and I have much to learn. Nevertheless, I feel that I should conclude this chapter with some personal observations on the guiding principles that I have followed so far. As I look back, I think there are three primary factors responsible for our growth: the call and purpose of God for my life; the purposes of God for Europe, Ukraine and the former Soviet Union; and most important, the grace of God.

Here are some other important factors:

- A high level of dedication and God centeredness
- Character, integrity and honesty with God and man
- Sound and powerful teaching of the Word
- Constant demonstration of the supernatural
- Social involvement of the church in society
- Strong structure and administration
- Recognition of women as equal partners in Christ for the harvest
- The ability to mobilize and motivate the church for action
- Strong and fervent prayer
- Freedom and an environment focused on individual fulfillment
- The ability to overcome cultural barriers
- Work, work and more work

CHAPTER THREE

SUSTAINING THE MOVE OF GOD

Mike Okonkwo

Mike Okonkwo is the presiding bishop of The Redeemed Evangelical Mission with over 150 branches worldwide. Okonkwo's Holy Spirit-inspired insight into the Word of God has been a tremendous inspiration to the millions around the globe who have been impacted by his message.

He is the host of the popular Power in the Word Network, *an international radio and television broadcast. Mike is an alumnus of the Morris Cerullo School of Ministry and of Covington Theological*

Seminary in the United States. He has several doctoral degrees and honorary awards. He is the convener of Communion of Covenant Ministers International, a coconvener of National Ministers Conference as well as the president of Pentecostal Fellowship of Nigeria.

Mike Okonkwo's wife is Peace Okonkwo, and they have been blessed with a daughter, Uche.

The apostle Paul had a special relationship with his protégé, Timothy. Timothy had become an essential link between Paul and the future. At one point, Paul said to Timothy, "The things that you have heard from me among many witnesses, commit these to faithful men who will be able to teach others also" (2 Tim. 2:2).

A STRUCTURE FOR CONTINUITY

In order for the move of God to be sustained from generation to generation, it goes without saying that there must be a structure for continuity. Paul knew that his generation must pass the baton to the next and that was why he mentored Timothy until he was confident that Timothy could represent him as a true "son" in the gospel. Not only did he mentor Timothy, but he also gave Timothy the tremendous responsibility of passing on to others the truths that Timothy had received.

This principle can be traced back to Genesis. Genesis 18:19 records God saying, "For I have known [Abraham], in order that he may command his children and his household after him, that they keep the way of the LORD, to do righteousness and justice, that the LORD may bring to Abraham what He has spoken to him." God literally was saying that Abraham needed to make sure that the generation coming after him would be aware of and continue in the move of God that began with their father, Abraham.

We also can take Moses, as he was leading the children of Israel out of Egypt, as an example. God gave clear instructions that everything the children of Israel experienced must be documented and frequently recited so that the generations to come would understand God's commandments and obey them (see Deut. 6:6-9,20-25).

Look at Elijah and Elisha. In the account of their ministry, we discover that Elisha simply followed Elijah everywhere for several years. Elisha was an understudy; he had no desire or intent to take over Elijah's ministry. I would venture to speculate that all Elisha had in mind was to assist Elijah in being everything that God had called him to be. However, in helping Elijah, he arrived at his own destiny (see 1 Kings 19:16—2 Kings 2). When you help someone arrive at his or her destiny, you open the door for ultimately arriving at yours.

A challenge facing the Body of Christ today is that we must not lose our grip on the biblical concept of mentoring. Too many people who are called by God tend to run off to do their own thing, submitting to no one and believing that they personally have all that they need. Is it not amazing that the world has tapped into the principle of networking to the extent that large companies are merging one with another and forming conglomerates, but the Body of Christ, rather than networking, is running solo? If there was ever a time that the Church must come together and speak with one voice throughout the nations of the world, it is now! For too long the Church has been singing diverse tunes, confusing the upcoming generation.

THE POWER OF THE WORD

I can say without fear of contradiction that, during the period of time when I came to know the Lord, knowledge of the Word of

God was scarce in Nigeria. Revival had just begun seeping into the country, and there were many distorted interpretations of the Word of God. At that time, the Pentecostal movement was largely known as a mushroom movement, meaning in Nigerian terminology that it was insignificant. That was because many Nigerians believed that all the Lord is interested in is our salvation. Once we are saved, our only focus from then on is getting into heaven. Few thought of their salvation as producing abundant life here and now. Another misperception was that pursuing excellence in any area should never be attempted; pursuing excellence was seen as carnal or worldly. Our slogan was "Repent or perish," and nothing more was to be added.

When I became a Christian, I continued for a time in the ignorance into which I had been indoctrinated. However, as I studied and prayed and matured, God began to open my eyes to the deeper truths of His Word. I began to realize that God's thoughts toward us are thoughts of peace and not of evil (see Jer. 29:11). I saw that every good and perfect gift comes from the Father of lights (see Jas. 1:17). I began to understand that the Word of God was powerful enough to put food on your table, clothes on your back and a shelter over your head. I discovered that the way to prosper and succeed in any area of life was by obeying the Word of God. Little wonder that God said to Joshua:

> This Book of the Law shall not depart from your mouth, but you shall meditate in it day and night, that you may observe to do according to all that is written in it. For then you will make your way prosperous, and then you will have good success (Josh. 1:8).

Having made these discoveries in the Bible, I developed two key principles that have continued to guide my life:

- Whatever the Word of God cannot give to me does not exist as far as I am concerned.
- Whatever the Word of God cannot give to me I obviously do not need.

A Mentor for Young Leaders

With this understanding in the back of my mind, I earnestly began to seek the face of the Lord concerning the move of God in Nigeria. I heard the Spirit of the Lord say that Nigeria would be pivotal in the end-time revival to come. As a young minister, I learned, with the apostle Paul, what it was to be abased and what it was to abound. I discovered the secret of success, and I came to realize that there is no glory without a story and no star without a scar. I committed myself to helping the Christian leaders of the upcoming generation maximize their potential and be all that the Lord has called them to be. This was born out of my conviction that no person can get the job done alone but that only together can we do it successfully. I began to interact more and more with the younger ministers, inviting them to my office, encouraging them and creating as many forums as possible to interact with them, to rejoice in their successes and to help them through their failures.

I was determined to follow the examples of Paul, Abraham, Moses and Elijah.

Pentecostal Fellowship of Nigeria

My convictions about discipling and mentoring young Christian leaders gave birth to the idea of a relationship-based networking organization. In conjunction with a few other friends, Pentecostal Fellowship of Nigeria (PFN) was born. Today, the membership of PFN has grown from fewer than a dozen churches to thousands. People have asked me how I cope with my responsibilities as the presiding bishop of The Redeemed Evangelical Mission, with numerous branches around the world, and as the president of PFN, with thousands of churches under it, and yet still find time for young ministries. To the many who ask, my answer has remained the same: I derive great personal satisfaction from watching young ministries grow in power and influence and seeing their fruits, not only in Nigeria, but also around the world. To me, this confirms the parable of Jesus in Matthew 13:31-32:

> Another parable He put forth to them, saying: "The kingdom of heaven is like a mustard seed, which a man took and sowed in his field, which indeed is the least of all the seeds; but when it is grown it is greater than the herbs and becomes a tree, so that the birds of the air come and nest in its branches."

What approach did I take toward establishing PFN?

Not surprisingly, the initial reaction of the younger ministers toward the new PFN was one of caution. A good number of the ministers were uncertain as to what I was hoping to achieve. They believed that they had little or nothing to offer an older, more visible leader like me. So I felt that the Lord was directing me to attend their conferences, not as a guest speaker, but simply as part of the audience. They were astonished. To their amazement, I would take copious notes while they were teaching, because I truly believed that through them God could speak fundamental truths to me that I had not heard before. When they saw me taking notes, they could hardly believe that there was something I could possibly learn from their teachings.

As time went by, however, these younger ministers began to discover that laboring together could release a power that would increase the corporate anointing on our different ministries. Gradually, the generational gap began to close, and they began to feel more comfortable in approaching me, knowing that I was more than ready to listen to them no matter what their challenge was.

Communion of Covenant Ministers International

I took the time to encourage and minister to the younger ministers even when they felt like failures. I showed them from personal example that errors and mistakes were not meant to be tombs but rather stepping-stones to greater heights. I started Communion of Covenant Ministers International (CCMI), inviting men and women with callings in different ministries to interact with me on a one-on-one basis and to fellowship together. I began to organize leadership seminars to provide opportunities for them to ask questions and to share their challenges. Today, CCMI continues as a network, bringing together various ministries in order to demonstrate that our strength lies in our diversity.

THE CHALLENGES OF PIONEERING

The desire to impact the upcoming generation became a driving force for me. In every one of the conferences I organized, I made it a point to emphasize the fact that obedience to God does not guarantee a challenge-free life. Jesus never promised a bed of roses; rather, He said in John 16:33, "In the world you will have tribulation; but be of good cheer, I have overcome the world." I would regularly share my personal experiences with them in order to encourage them to take decisive action whenever they were certain of what the Word of God was saying in their specific situation, irrespective of the popular opinion of the day.

The Ordination of Women

A clear example of this was the challenge I encountered when God began speaking to me about the ordination of women. At that time, the general belief was that women must remain silent in the church; only men could qualify for positions of leader-ship. However, I knew that God had spoken to my heart. There were many examples of women leaders in the Bible, which, to my mind, validated the ordination of women. However, many people within the Church were not ready to accept it.

I knew that I needed to stand firm on the Word. I trusted God to bring to pass all that He had said concerning the ministry of women, especially since I saw clearly the hand of God on some of the women around me, including my wife. I knew the call of God was strong upon her, but ordaining women was not permitted. In spite of this, I took a bold step and publicly ordained some women to the gospel ministry. This, as might be expected, generated a lot of controversy, but I truly believed that if it was of God, it would stand. Today, the ministry of women remains. International Women's Prayer Conference, which started as a small gathering of women in our ministry, has now spread to other parts of the country and, indeed, to other nations of the world. The rest is history. Women now stand at the helm of both churches and ministries of great repute.

Prosperity

Even while I was still dealing with strong opposition to women in leadership, I received a further revelation from the Lord: Pastors do not have to be poor simply because they are pastors. I soon began teaching pastors from the Word of God about this. It was not long before I discovered that the more we taught this truth from the Word, the more we actually prospered materially. This provoked a new wave of opposition. But suddenly, pastors who had previously been disparaged as "mushrooms" (poor and insignificant) were now accused of being extravagant. I like to say that today, instead of being "mushrooms," we pastors have become "much-rooms."

Marketing and Media

Those weren't the only innovations I felt were needed in the Body of Christ. For one thing, I did not believe that the gospel was spreading fast enough in Nigeria. What could be done to speed it up?

As a first step, I began an aggressive marketing campaign so that people would become more aware of what God was capable of doing if they served Him faithfully. I believed that we owed the world in which we live a more accurate and appealing picture of God. This led to our putting up billboards and using various other forms of advertising. The driving force behind the marketing campaign was that none should go to hell out of ignorance. Even if someone had never heard a preacher, we tried to be sure that he or she would have at least seen an advertisement. With that, the opposition increased once again. Many who did not understand the move of God believed we had gone off the deep end. However, today almost 30 percent of billboards in major cities throughout Nigeria advertise Jesus. The Word is getting out!

We also realized that there was still an untapped medium through which we could gain access to homes: electronic media. Even though its use as an evangelistic tool was not yet widely accepted in Nigeria, I decided to step out in faith and exploit television with *Power in the Word Network*. This was during a time when the general belief that living the abundant life implied becoming entangled with the world still prevailed. I was severely verbally attacked for using television as a medium, but I knew that God had spoken. I also knew that all I needed to do was to stand my ground and that others would soon follow because the fruit of the ministry would speak for itself.

It was not long before testimonies of men and women who were saved, healed and delivered through *Power in the Word Network* began to filter in. Many other ministries then came to realize that, rather than being the devil's box, television could actually be a powerful tool of evangelism. Today, television ministry in Nigeria is aired by satellite and it reaches millions across all of Africa. Thousands are testifying of salvation and healing that have come through this ministry.

Relevant Music

As a lover of music, I encouraged the introduction of contemporary worship in all our services. While I am fond of hymns and we include the traditional organ in our services, I quickly embraced vibrant praise of contemporary worship with musical instruments such as drums, congas, kickers, trumpets and saxophones. The initial reaction was resistance, but we persisted, knowing that a lot of young people felt that traditional music was a bore; they preferred to go to clubs and discotheques for the kind of music they really enjoyed. And as a result of adding contemporary worship, many young people were drawn to our churches. Today, they are happy to express themselves in the language they understand within the confines of the church, rather than on the streets. Most Bible-believing churches in Nigeria are now filled with these same young people who are on fire for Jesus Christ.

I have come to a major conclusion through all these experiences: Whatever can be validated with the Word of God can be done. No matter what the challenge is and how uncharted the waters may be, God is in the business of using the foolish things of the world to confound the wise. However, I must sound a note of caution here and say that rather than running with every new idea, we must test every spirit (see 1 John 4:1). Every word *from* God must be validated with the Word *of* God. That is the litmus test.

TRANSPARENCY BEFORE THE NEXT GENERATION

In sustaining the move of God, there is a need to be aware of the next generation. There is a mighty army looking up to us, ready and willing to walk in our steps. If there is anything that we should endeavor to do for this group of people, it is not just to show them our glory but also to go a step further and tell them our story. We must tell them about those times when we were discouraged so that they may know that truly "Elijah was a man with a nature like ours" (Jas. 5:17); this will no doubt encourage them.

There is a tendency for people to think that they have done all that there is to do and that they have nothing else to contribute. There is also a tendency for the young up-and-coming ministers to feel threatened by the successes of their mentors. This is not a new thing; it happened to Joshua. Joshua had followed Moses over the years. He had seen Moses strike the rock and water come gushing out. He had seen Moses part the Red Sea. He had seen incredible miracles, and then suddenly Moses turned to him and anointed him to take over (see Num. 27:22-23). The logical thing would have been for Joshua to pray for Moses to live long enough to finish what he started. After all, God Himself testified of Moses that of all men who lived, there was none other with whom He spoke face-to-face (see Num. 12:6-8). So Joshua had good reason to feel intimidated by the achievements of Moses.

I believe that God saw Joshua's fear and his seeming insecurity when faced with the challenge of leadership. That was why in the first chapter of Joshua, God kept encouraging Joshua not to be afraid and reassured him that as He had been with Moses, so He would also be with him. If the record set by Moses had not intimidated Joshua, God would not have needed to continually remind him that the miracle worker was not Moses, but God Himself. What matters is not who you are but whose you are and what He can make out of you.

> *We must not hide our battle scars from our successors. Our testimony of moving through difficulty might provide just the strength they require to arrive at the destiny God has mapped out for them.*

In the book of Deuteronomy (which can be considered Moses' transfer-of-power document), Moses took time to analyze all the events of the previous years, highlighting even his own weaknesses so that Joshua and the children of Israel could learn from them. We must not hide our battle scars from our successors. Our testimony of moving through difficulty might provide just the strength they require to arrive at the destiny God has mapped out for them. Moses was not ashamed to explain the reason why he could not enter the Promised Land, because he knew that someone would learn from it and would not have to die in the wilderness as he did.

The sooner we realize that we have failed in our task if the generation coming after us does not do greater exploits than we do, the better. The reason why we waded through our mighty rivers and were not drowned was so that we could make a path for the people following us on the road to success. Many have unwittingly painted a picture of ministry as bliss so that today

are falling by the wayside in search of bliss without
owhere in the Word of God is this promised.

WOUNDED SOLDIERS

There is a dire need in our generation to assist our wounded soldiers in getting back on their feet. The fact that believers fall is
not the greatest challenge; the greatest challenge is whether we
are able to help them get back up. Micah 7:8 states: "Do not
rejoice over me, my enemy; when I fall, I will arise; when I sit in
darkness, the LORD will be a light to me." While I agree that we
must not endorse a license to sin, this Scripture encourages us
not to die in the error we may commit. Proverbs 24:16 says, "For
a righteous man may fall seven times and rise again, but the
wicked shall fall by calamity."

Obviously then, the problem is not simply in falling; it is
also in not rising again. Many people today have killed the
wounded soldiers in an attempt to maintain an appearance of
holiness. Beloved, step back and take a journey in your mind's
eye along the road you have traveled so far. You might be
shocked to discover that some of the things for which you are
criticizing others are the same pitfalls you encountered on your
road to success and for which God restored you.

We have been called into the ministry of reconciliation. This
call has caused me to draw close to many ministers of God to the
point where they could confess their faults to me and receive
godly counsel, knowing that their secrets remained safe. I knew
that if they trusted me enough to share their challenges with me,
I had the responsibility to cover them, counsel them, pray with
them and help them get back on their feet so that they could
continue what God had called them to do. To the glory of God,
testimonies abound of many who might have fallen away from
ministry but who, through our relationships, became strong

once again and who today are on the forefront, doing exploits for the Kingdom.

Paul, writing to Philemon, admitted that Onesimus had missed the mark—he had done what was wrong. But Paul said,

> I appeal to you for my son Onesimus, whom I have begotten while in my chains, who once was unprofitable to you, but now is profitable to you and to me (Philem. 1:10-11).

We could easily say, "But, Paul, Onesimus should be punished. Don't you know what he did?" Yes, Paul knew, but Paul also remembered how far the Lord had brought him. In 1 Timothy 1:12-16, he did a brief recap:

> And I thank Christ Jesus our Lord who has enabled me, because He counted me faithful, putting me into the ministry, although I was formerly a blasphemer, a persecutor, and an insolent man; but I obtained mercy because I did it ignorantly in unbelief. And the grace of our Lord was exceedingly abundant, with faith and love which are in Christ Jesus. This is a faithful saying and worthy of all acceptance, that Christ Jesus came into the world to save sinners, of whom I am chief. However, for this reason I obtained mercy, that in me first Jesus Christ might show all longsuffering, as a pattern to those who are going to believe on Him for everlasting life.

If you remind yourself from where you've come, not to wallow in self-pity, but to motivate yourself to move ahead, you will discover that there is nothing others have done for which they do not also deserve forgiveness.

Let me finally illustrate this point with the following verses in Galatians. Paul expressly says,

> Brethren, if a man is overtaken in any trespass, you who are spiritual restore such a one in a spirit of gentleness, considering yourself lest you also be tempted. Bear one another's burdens, and so fulfill the law of Christ (6:1-2).

In other words, clean up the wounded soldiers, bind up their wounds and help them recover quickly. When they are strong, you will also be strong.

PRINCIPLES TO TEACH THE NEXT GENERATION

Take time to disciple the people God has brought to you. Impact their lives and be sure to deposit in them all that God has put into you. You are only a success when you have a successor. Like

Take time to disciple the people God has brought to you. Impact their lives and be sure to deposit in them all that God has put into you.

Paul, we can say, "I have fought a good fight, I have finished my course, I have kept the faith" (2 Tim. 4:7) only when we have successfully trained men and women who can take to a higher level our work of allowing the gospel to impact people's lives. The following are some principles about sustaining the move of God that you may want to teach your disciples; these principles will benefit them greatly.

God Demands Excellence

In sustaining the current move of God in Nigeria, we must remember to conduct ourselves in an appropriate, businesslike manner. In the early days of the Pentecostal movement in Nigeria, everything was taken for granted. Everything was based on a loose system of verbal trust; very little, if anything, was documented. This fell short of the excellence that God demands of us. Just as all secular professions (medical, legal, accounting and so on) have standards for members of their professional bodies to uphold, so God also has a standard for His servants. This truth is especially relevant today, since some believers have taken hold of an exaggerated principle of liberty, concluding that they do not need to be accountable to anyone. But liberty is not a license to sin: "For you, brethren, have been called to liberty; only do not use liberty as an opportunity for the flesh, but through love serve one another" (Gal. 5:13).

Seeing this need, I began to organize management seminars in which we took a business approach to the corporate side of ministry. I began to require that each ministry have an established corporate office. Each leader needed to schedule and allow time for appointments. Every minister had to show up on time for all scheduled programs, setting an example in this and in everything else he or she did. Excellence became the watchword.

Initially, because of the influences of our culture, this level of discipline appeared difficult to apply, particularly for the new move we were experiencing in the country. Many sought reasons for me to relax the rules, but I have remained firm. Today, having waded through some turbulent waters, ministries that learned and practiced these principles are grateful to me for that training, and their leaders would not have it any other way.

Character Must Balance the Anointing

So much emphasis in modern ministry is placed on the anointing. People seeking an increase in their anointing are willing to make almost any sacrifice to attend seminars and conferences in order to receive it. While I have no problem with that, we must also realize that there is a fine balance between anointing and character. May I suggest that though the anointing will open the door, it is your character that will ultimately sustain you and your ministry. No matter how great you are today in the kingdom of God, get ready, because without integrity, you are going down! Too many who have emerged in ministry have been written down in history as good starters, but when they were catapulted into the limelight, they suddenly ceased to exist. This has become a regular occurrence in the Body of Christ and has brought with it a great deal of reproach.

God is a good God. He is not planning to use you today and dump you tomorrow. He is a consistent God. He delights in the prosperity of His servants, and His joy is to see us increase in that which He has committed into our hands. God is not intimidated by our successes, nor is He paralyzed by our failure. Paul, writing to Timothy, his son in the faith, considered it a privilege to be a minister: "And I thank Christ Jesus our Lord who has enabled me, because He counted me faithful, putting me into the ministry" (1 Tim. 1:12).

Every Member Is a Minister

The call to ministry is not just for the fivefold minister (see Eph. 4:11), nor is it restricted to people with nice-sounding titles. Rather, it is a call that includes every believer. Once this idea became clear, I joined with others to organize National Ministers' Conference (NMC). The purpose of NMC is to impact the upcoming generation. We specifically desired to counteract a fast-spreading error in Nigeria. Some Pentecostal leaders were teaching that just about everyone who wanted to serve the Lord as a minister of the gospel needed to be either an apostle, prophet, evangelist, pastor or teacher. Titles became a major emphasis, overshadowing the actual work of the ministry. To win a soul, therefore, you had to have the title "evangelist"; and to pray for the sick, you had to be recognized as a healer.

The craving for titles became so inordinate that we began to teach two sessions on ministerial ethics in all of our conferences so that the ministers would recognize that servanthood and changed lives—not titles—validated their ministry. I am a firm believer in the fact that God wants all things done decently and in order (see 1 Cor. 14:40). However, the Word of God states clearly that signs should follow every believer, not just those with titles (see Mark 16:17-18).

Each One Is Unique

In light of this overemphasis on titles, we began to remind believers that each of us has a specific assignment and that God has given us the necessary tools and gifts to carry it out. So rather than trying to be like Brother Mike, we each need to maintain our unique individuality and be who God made us to be. This is the path toward becoming the greatest achievers of all time. I also began to teach a new definition of success: doing what God has called you to do, and doing it well. These principles have gone a long way to help the younger generation thrive in their God-given strengths, rather than wither in the fruitless process of imitating another person.

We Are Accountable to God for Our Talents

In Jesus' parable of the talents in Matthew 25:14-30, the master gave talents to each of his servants according to his ability. This shows us that God is not a taskmaster and will not overload us with something we cannot handle. If God has called you, it is because He already knows that you have all that it takes to succeed. He knows you much better than you know yourself.

The master also gave his servants free will to do as they wanted. When the master returned from his journey, he called the servants to give account of their activities while he was away. In the same way, there will be a day for each of us to give an account of how we have conducted ourselves and carried out our assignments. The first two servants gave their report to the master with joy, while the third one blamed the master for his woes rather than looking inward and repenting. My prayer is that we will be like the first two servants who met their master with joy and earned his commendation:

> Well done, good and faithful servant; you have been faithful over a few things, I will make you ruler over many things. Enter into the joy of your Lord (Matt. 25:23).

Unfortunately, many servants of God who started well have been cut off before their time because they lacked integrity. We must learn from their successes as well as their failures in order to keep history from repeating itself. When God calls, He desires our success, but it must be based on His standards and not ours.

Integrity Is Essential
As I have already mentioned, we are not all called to fivefold ministry, but every believer is a minister. God's standard is the same for those standing behind the pulpit as it is for those sitting in the pews. The standards are not far-fetched; they are all rooted in the Word of God. In order to sustain the move of God, we must abide by these standards; and one very key factor is integrity.

"Integrity" is an all-encompassing word. The word "integrity" implies honesty, perfection, soundness, uprightness, righteousness, fairness and prudence. Unfortunately, this word is a far cry from what we often see in ministry today. Suddenly, we begin laying more emphasis on signs, wonders and miracles than we do on integrity. I believe this is a trick of the devil to discredit Christian ministries. Remember the words of Jesus Himself in Matthew 7:22-23:

> Many will say to Me in that day, "Lord, Lord, have we not prophesied in Your name, cast out demons in Your name, and done many wonders in Your name?" And then I will declare to them, "I never knew you; depart from Me, you who practice lawlessness!"

We need to consider the biblical principles that guide our ministries and adhere strictly to them. Let us consider a certain man of God, whom God raised up outside the lineage of Eli to be a prophet in the land. This man ruled the nation of Israel for many years; and when he was about to be replaced by a king, he declared with boldness:

> Here I am. Witness against me before the LORD and before His anointed: Whose ox have I taken, or whose donkey have I taken, or whom have I cheated? Whom have I oppressed, or from whose hand have I received any bribe with which to blind my eyes? I will restore it to you (1 Sam. 12:3).

These were the words of the prophet Samuel. I do not know about you, but I love to seek out those who have made a positive impact in ministry in order to learn from them. Conversely, I look at those who have fallen in order to learn how to avoid their mistakes. Samuel was a prophet in Israel. He grew up in the house of Eli and was a witness to the atrocities of the children of Eli. He saw them feed on evil, and he also watched God's reaction to the situation. Notice that Eli's sons were God's choice. Earlier on, God had informed Moses that the children of Aaron would serve as priests in His Temple indefinitely. But when it was time for Eli's children to take over the priesthood, God cut them off. Samuel witnessed all this, and I believe that was what moved him to purpose in his heart to walk in integrity.

Integrity does not only pertain to the big things. If you also do not maintain integrity in an area as seemingly insignificant as your daily appointments, it will be difficult for you to maintain integrity in the area of your finances or even your marriage. Do not try to isolate integrity; make it a way of life. Take time to find out what is expected of you by the government of the country where you have been called to serve. Follow all the rules that have been laid down. When you have questions, employ the services of legal counsel. Keep all your paperwork and documention in a safe place, and let everything important be documented. Find out about the tax laws, and keep good accounting records. This should be the standard from day one. Don't plan to start these habits later, because tomorrow will be too late.

Many Christians find financial and legal accountability very difficult. We would rather operate strictly on the principle of trust. As ideal as this sounds, we still need to exercise some caution, since many Christians have been burned because they did not take time to document things properly. Remember that this treasure is in earthen (fallible human) vessels. No matter how honest the people around you may appear to be, if there are no records, there is no proof of their integrity.

CONCLUSION

This chapter represents some of the practical lessons I have learned as a minister. They will aid us not only in sustaining the move of God in Nigeria but also in taking the gospel to other nations. As a result of the visible positive impact of many ministries in our nation, God has opened doors in other nations, not just to establish branches of Nigerian-based ministries, but also to train leaders of other nations so that they can impact their nations for Jesus Christ.

CHAPTER FOUR

DEALING WITH THE DEMONIC

Ayo Oritsejafor

Ayo Oritsejafor is a renowned preacher, pastor and evangelist, with a clear anointing of God upon his life. In 1972, he gave his life to the Lord and, during a crusade, was miraculously delivered from demonic influence associated with traditional African religion. Almost immediately, Ayo felt a call of God on his life and enrolled in New Covenant Bible Institute in Benin City, Nigeria.

Since then his anointed messages have brought salvation, deliverance, revival, healing and outstanding miracles to thousands across the world as God's power is demonstrated with signs and wonders. As a keynote speaker, he has ministered in crusades, with well over 2 million people in attendance at a single service. He has also ministered in various conferences and seminars in over 45 countries around the world.

In 1980, in a bid to fulfill God's mandate, Ayo started a television program called Hour of Deliverance. *Various television stations in Nigeria, as well as in Europe, are currently carrying this program—still airing after more than 20 years—with a potential viewing audience of around 64 million people.*

As a prolific writer, he has authored several books, which include Walking in Unity, Power Through the Church, The Battle Is in the Mind, Be an Overcomer, Power for the Journey, Faith Antidote for Daily Living, A Voice in the Wilderness *and* A Man Amongst Men.

Because of the apostolic call upon Ayo, his ministry acts as a covering to several ministries in Africa, Europe and the United States. Ayo is married and resides in Warri, Nigeria, with his wife, Helen, and their family.

Throughout my many years of ministry, I have observed and experienced a tremendously important truth: The spiritual world controls the physical world, either for good or evil (see 2 Cor. 10:3-4; Eph. 6:12). God, through His Church activated by the Holy Spirit, seeks to steer human events toward the values of His kingdom. At the same time, multitudes of evil ruling spirits seek to thwart the progress of God's work as well as hinder the well-being of nations. Nigeria serves as a perfect model of this constant battle of good versus evil. Word of Life Bible Church, the church that I pastor, based in Warri, Nigeria, has found itself in the forefront of this battle largely because of geography.

The ruling spirits in the region of southern Nigeria where our ministry is located fall loosely into three categories, namely *marine spirits, witchcraft spirits* and *bloodthirsty spirits* (violence and destruction). These ruling spirits take on different names in various communities and tribes, but they operate in basically the same way: They seek to draw the inhabitants of the land into covenants with the multiple gods that the people worship. Their ultimate goal is to take control of the territory in which they operate.

These spirits invariably govern the lives and lifestyles of the people. The influence of these ruling powers explains territorial behavior (why people from certain tribes act in a certain manner), e.g., drunkenness, immorality, anger, divorce and so on. Different towns and communities have ancient altars and juju (our name for the occult powers that the communities have subjected themselves to). This virtual cocktail of occult powers dominates the landscape in the southern part of Nigeria where we are located.

Those who are possessed by these spirits have certain taboos and superstitions (extremely common in this part of the world) to which they strictly adhere. Some of them, for example, will never wear anything red—clothes, jewelry or shoes. Others abstain from eating certain types of food ordinarily eaten in their region. Others are not permitted to look into mirrors. The list goes on. A common practice in our section of the country is body marking (making cuts on the face and various other parts of the body), which the Bible prohibits (see Lev. 19:28). This is more serious than tattooing, since not only is it indelible but it also carries severe spiritual consequences. These tribal markings are an attempt by the ruling spirits to make the statement "You are permanently mine!"

MARINE SPIRITS

Marine spirits rule many communities, since most towns and villages in our region are located in areas crisscrossed by rivers. The manifestation of the working of these marine spirits is evi-

dent in the high level of sexual immorality and unstable marriages found in these areas. Although marine spirits manifest
themselves differently in different Nigerian communities and
take different names, they are one and the same. The worship of
Mami Wata, the ruling spirit over the territory, is permeated by
sexual perversion and ritual sacrifice.

In our ministry, we have helped many young girls who had
been gripped by the spirit of prostitution. First prostitutes in
Nigeria, these girls ended up working as prostitutes on the streets
of Europe, especially in Italy, after being deceived by the false
promise of financial prosperity in Europe. Many of them have
found deliverance in our ministry through speaking God's Word.
It is evident that there are ruling spirits at work, since these victims are predominantly from the same geographic region. The
problem is so endemic that the Nigerian government has set up
a department to handle this problem on a full-time basis. Many
of these girls take charms and amulets, which they receive from
local witch doctors, abroad with them—all in an effort to enhance
their attractiveness. They also continue to make sacrifices even in
foreign lands! This is an example of how strong the Mami Wata
spirit can be, producing unleashed sexual immorality.

The Mami Wata sexual immorality, which has manifested
itself in prostitution both locally and internationally, gained
ascendancy in Nigeria only in the late 1980s. In the natural, this
rise was attributed to high unemployment and a subsequent
mass exodus of young professionals to foreign nations in search
of a more ordered existence. This emigration was indirectly
caused by a failing economy.

A publication released by the public affairs section of the
United States Embassy, dated April 6, 2000, estimated that
over 1 million women and children were being trafficked
around the world each year. Over 50,000 of them were sold
into the United States alone. In Western Europe, the estimate

was a whopping 500,000 women a year.

The reality, according to an article released by the President's Interagency Council on Women in the United States, is that trafficking in women and children is the third largest profit source for organized crime, the first two being drugs and guns. Profit for female trafficking worldwide is computed in billions of dollars; and in trafficking of Nigerian girls to Europe, it is estimated that a trafficker can expect a return of $50,000 for every girl successfully delivered.

Seduction and Jealousy

Many of those who are possessed by these powerful marine spirits are adept at seduction. These ladies, just by their looks and with their eyes, know how to seduce an otherwise unwilling, responsible man who is spiritually inept. They do not hesitate to go into homes and break up marriages. As can well be imagined, the resulting high divorce rate has its attendant problems, including unstable and problematic children.

Through many years of personal counseling with such seductive women, I have found out that many of them have "spirit husbands." These women's problems begin to manifest themselves only after the women get married, provoking their spirit husbands (demons) to become jealous. For example, the wedding ring of a lady disappeared mysteriously. Through prayer and counseling it came to light that she had had a spirit husband who had been having sexual intercourse with her before she got married. She had first entered into this demonic marriage covenant not by her own choice but by having been dedicated to the Mami Wata spirit cult as a child.

Barrenness and AIDS

Many instances of barrenness without medical explanation have been linked directly to the intervention of these dark ruling spirits. Married women who have directly or inadvertently made pacts with Mami Wata spirits are often visited at night by their spirit husbands. In their dreams, these women often see themselves playing with or having sexual intercourse with snakes. If they were pregnant prior to this visitation, they often will lose the baby through a miscarriage. This cycle repeats itself—no matter how many times they become pregnant. These unexplained miscarriages naturally put such strain on the marriage that it is eventually destroyed. These divorces are considered inevitable, especially in a society that places great value on a woman's ability to bear children. Like other emissaries of Satan, Mami Wata spirits come to steal, to kill and to destroy.

Another severe consequence of the operation of this ruling marine spirit is the scourge of sexually transmitted diseases, not the least of which is the AIDS virus. Pick up any Nigerian newspaper and witness the callous way in which the devil is destroying lives through sexually transmitted diseases. Demographic anaylyses have shown, not surprisingly, that a high percentage of AIDS victims in Nigeria are from these river areas, the strongholds of Mami Wata.

Their Power Source

How do these marine spirits attain such power? Their stronghold of dominance over the people is greatly increased through idolatrous worship. These spirits, under the guise of being intermediaries to God on behalf of the people, demand worship. Spirit worship is closely related to ancestral worship, which is so common in African culture. Most communities or villages in this region worship objects (usually carved from wood); or they revere certain objects such as trees, rocks and hills that traditionally have had certain mystic powers attributed to them. To the untrained observer the carvings merely appear to be works of art. However, the truth is that through sacrifices to and worship directed toward these inanimate objects, the people dedicate themselves to the ruling territorial spirit in the area, Mami Wata. Unwittingly, people have made themselves servants of the devil through this practice (see Rom. 6:16).

The marine spirits ruling under Mami Wata strengthen and maintain their hold on communities from generation to generation through the practice of childhood initiation. When children are born, they are taken to the river, where they are put through a ceremony of initiation; from that point on they are dedicated to the spirits that occupy certain shrines. Sadly, they go through most of their lives in torment and misery.

Most of these villages conduct state festivals in which every resident (including visitors from other countries who happen to be there) must participate. These festivals serve as avenues for the ruling marine spirits to perpetuate their grip on the people. Sadly, too many people (including educated people and even university professors) interpret these festivals as a reflection of our culture and rich heritage. During these festivals, which may last up to a week, the presiding high priest makes incantations and sacrifices purported to bless the people and the land! (Has anyone ever heard of the devil blessing people?) There are usually several ceremonies during which meals are prepared and shared communally—perverted counterfeits of the biblical injunction of the breaking of bread, or Holy Communion. Evil communion is conducted in this case! Through the celebration of these festivals and the sharing of unholy communion, whole communities and generations of people open themselves to possession and oppression by these evil powers. Tremendous social pressure is brought to bear on those unwilling to participate in these demonic festivals. In many cases they are ostracized. Yes, even in modern-day

Nigeria! With great regularity multitudes of desensitized people stream to the rivers with live animals, food, drinks, clothes and so on to appease and worship the Mami Wata gods by throwing or pouring these items into the river.

The Challenge for the Church

The Church has taken a stand against this filthy power of darkness. The voice of the Church both inside and outside the country is beginning to stem the tide. I have had the opportunity to minister to many Nigerians in these situations, and I have seen people set free and begin to live responsible lives. For example, a lady was set free from the spirit of prostitution while she was watching my TV program, *Hour of Deliverance*. She immediately packed her personal belongings and left her partner in the hotel room, scorning the prospect of making money that night. She found her way to the church compound, where she immediately received counseling and deliverance. That night she gave her life to the Lord and never went back to the streets. As a result of numerous encounters like this, God has led me to establish a deliverance school where troubled souls can come to be freed from demonic spirits and to be discipled.

Presently, we have embarked on an educational program in which a healthy Christian environment is provided for academic pursuits ranging from elementary school education to university-level studies. Education helps to curb ignorance of the spiritual environment in which we live and consequently puts the future of our nation back into the hands of our educated youth. This project was born out of my strong belief that a large part of our battle is against ignorance. The Bible teaches that it is the knowledge of the truth that brings freedom (see John 8:32). I am a firm believer that godly education will open the doors for a prosperous future.

WITCHCRAFT SPIRITS

The second ruling spirit that has sought to hinder the spread of the gospel in the southern region of Nigeria is the spirit of witchcraft. Witchcraft has been in existence in these communities for a long time. Through our ministry experience, we have discovered that many people enter into witchcraft deliberately. Their stated purpose is either to destroy the lives and dreams of people that they dislike or to actualize certain goals for themselves.

Their Mode of Operation

These loathsome spirits operate clandestinely. They work essentially at night and frequently take on human form, since people would be more likely to stay clear of them if they were to appear in their true forms, with their true names. Although most people say that they reject the practice of witchcraft, they ignorantly consult with native doctors, sorcerers, charmers, necromancers and diviners. Many have been misled to believe that these supposedly innocent practices have nothing to do with witchcraft; consequently, these practices are commonplace in markets and other such public places.

Others are aware of the dangers these practices pose, but many feel helpless in the face of such an onslaught of evil. They know that dabbling in the occult and specifically in witchcraft is not harmless fun, contrary to the thinking of some Christians in the West who regard certain manifestations of the occult as benign. I am amazed that some Christians are still arguing about the appropriateness of their children watching the recently released Harry Potter movies, which are designed to make evil look like fun. Some are so deceived that they think they can love both Jesus and Harry Potter at the same time! I heard that a recent survey of American youth reveals that approximately 90 percent consider the practice of witchcraft harmless! Nigerians, on the other hand, for most of their lives have seen up close the destructive work of this evil ruling spirit of witchcraft.

The witches in the southern part of Nigeria do not have sophisticated methods of operation. They do not hold conferences in hotels, march publicly or fight for the right to hold open gatherings; nor do they recruit through websites. Witches are not publicly accepted by entire communities. Their method of operation borders on the bizarre, as they often meet in nonphysical form on treetops, rooftops and other such outlandish places. These, in fact, are their covens!

The rites of initiation into witchcraft are often transferred generationally from parents or relatives. Transference commonly takes place through eating certain specially prepared foods. It can be extremely difficult to reject initiation, since it is carried out by people who are loved and trusted. Schools and other such public institutions are also fertile ground for recruiting potential witches.

Witchcraft Exposed

One of the banes of Africa, and especially southern Nigeria, is the fact that we have practiced consulting the devil through spiritually blind native doctors. The Scriptures make clear the disastrous consequences of such an unwise choice (see Matt. 15:14). This, in part, explains why Nigeria has continued to wallow in darkness for so long. However, I continually thank God for His grace upon our land over the past few decades. Light is beginning to break through at last!

Our ministry, among many others, has accurately identified these spirits in our various regions, exposing them for what they really are. We are succeeding in making it very uncomfortable for them to continue their ungodly work. Through sound biblical teaching, effective counseling and demonic deliverance, we have continued to expose their hidden works. Knowledge of the truth is so important because these spirits maintain their strongholds largely through the exploitation of people's ignorance of God's Word. Countless numbers of people have now experienced freedom through attending our deliverance school, which is hosted on a regular basis at our church. Our 24/7 prayer chain also is a great help toward neutralizing the activities of witches in our region.

BLOODTHIRSTY SPIRITS

The third of the ruling spirits usually hides under the façade of intertribal and fratricidal wars. They succeed in producing undue agitation and general chaos that eventually manifest themselves in ritual killings.

African societies, and indeed most cultures the world over, have experienced one form of war or another. Bosnia, the Middle East, Northern Ireland and Chechnya, among many others, are all current reminders of this fact. On the surface, it would appear that one war is no different from another: Each is an attempted resolution of people's suspicions and age-old prejudices. However, in each case, there is an underlying spiritual root. That root is obvious in most African wars. In Nigeria I have identified altars and shrines intentionally dedicated to the worship of spirits who instigate and propagate these wars. The ultimate goal of these spirits of violence is death and destruction; they seek to impede progress and keep a people divided. Many of their altars are located in forests. These forests, crisscrossed by rivers, provide ideal locations for these spirits, since the abundance of water has created the vast rain forest of southern Nigeria.

During typical tribal wars, the high priest or native doctor consults the gods of war and supposedly receives power and direction. In return for victory, these ruling spirits make demands on the people to kill humans and bring the severed heads as sacrifices to their altars. The spirits' promise of protecting the community from attacks and destruction is so valued by the people that the price of human sacrifice is not too high.

Rites of Initiation

The ruling powers of violence and bloodletting perpetuate their hold over communities and tribes through the promise of continuous protection. People are initiated into offering sacrifice and worship at the spirits' shrines and altars when they seek protection from guns, machetes and poison during times of war. Indeed some actually become immune to machete cuts, gunshot wounds and poisons when they submit to these ruling spirits. I know that this will be hard for many Western readers of this book to believe, but it is a fact. The promise of supernatural protection often results in the initiation and baptism of whole communities at these altars.

Different tribes and communities in Nigeria have certain gods of war with whom they make unholy covenant. One group may worship the god of thunder; another group may worship the god of whirlwinds; and yet another may worship the god of iron. In times of war, the inhabitants of a whole town may visit their altars to offer sacrifice and oblation with the aim of gaining advantage over the opposing community or tribe. Unknown to these tribes is the fact that these ruling powers are all working together in unity. The ruling powers desire war and blood, so over the years they have conspired to cause tribal wars. Multitudes of otherwise innocent people are forced into idol worship—serving demons with human sacrifices—when they, along with the rest of their tribe, turn to gods in times of war. Their belief in this false promise of invincibility is not unlike that of the Philistine giant Goliath, who believed that his gods of war would deliver Israel into his hands (see 1 Sam. 17:43).

Demonic Chaos

A crisis that engulfed the city of Warri, where our church is located, illustrates the spiritual source of war in Nigeria. In 1995-96,
we suffered a fratricidal war, resulting in the tragic loss of lives
and property. Observers proposed different reasons for the war
and wanton destruction. Many suggested that it was a result of
the government's neglect of the region and the high incidence of
unemployment that ensued. Others insisted it emerged from
deep-seated prejudices and political manipulation. Behind all of
these natural manifestations, though, were the ruling forces of
darkness, the gods of this world, and specifically bloodthirsty
demons and altars.

A general atmosphere of violence and destruction became
rife when those altars demanded nothing short of human blood.
Even the youth became extremely militant and violent and
began to incite chaos. Incidents of kidnapping and hostage taking of expatriate oil workers were rampant. Ritual killings
became commonplace, and general chaos put this area in the
news on a daily basis. It was a period when people sought for
hope and direction and desperately needed answers.

The situation came to a head when scores of houses were
burned and a multitude of individuals were killed in just one
day. A state of emergency was declared, and our nation's president had to personally go to Warri to intervene and stop the
destruction. The army was sent to the region and a curfew was
enforced. A shoot-on-sight order was instituted. The enemy
was having a field day. The situation was so bad that there was
tribal tension even among Christians; factions were being
carved along tribal lines, because many believers failed to recognize the real enemy. This is the way that the spirit of violence
and bloodthirsty demons customarily work; and disappoint-
ingly, so many Christians could not recognize it for what it
was! The god of this world had blinded their eyes from seeing

that a major tactic of this ruling power is to engender mistrust and disunity among Christians, thereby hindering the work of the Kingdom.

The Church in the Gap

During this period, the local church I pastor, Word of Life Bible Church, made frantic efforts to bring peace to the war-torn area through a series of prayer meetings designed specifically to counter the efforts of these ugly demonic spirits and through several meetings with the leaders of the various tribes involved in the conflict. We established multiple prayer altars in the church, and later we continued to lead initiatives for peace meetings to promote unity among the feuding tribes and ethnic groups. In addition, the church financially assisted businesses that were ravaged through this tribal war. Many rental homes were provided for the displaced; food, clothing, medical aid and so on were given to those in need. While many churches closed down during this period, by the grace of God we experienced a surge in our attendance. This story, which told of the significant impact that our prayers and assistance were making on the region, was featured on both the BBC and CNN.

It was during these inauspicious times that the Lord asked me to build and dedicate a house of worship that seats 35,000 people. This grand building, dedicated by Morris Cerullo, became a symbol of hope, not just to the common person, but also to the many whose businesses were on the verge of collapsing and the capital investors whose investments were losing value by the day. The remarkable thing is that this multimillion dollar building project was completed during a season of severe crisis and war. Even more remarkable is the fact that this building was not located in one of the larger cities in Nigeria but in a city with only half a million people. It is an eloquent testimony to the fact that God can deliver people from the ruling powers of darkness and violence in order to make them vessels of honor to fulfill His plans and purposes.

During this period of severe crisis, many prominent Nigerians called me to say that because of the miraculous completion of our worship center, their faith was strengthened in God's ability to take care of His own. To them the church building was an unassailable beacon of hope. Noteworthy is the fact that some of those people who called were not Christians! Because of the hope that our ministry was bringing to the community, many businesses decided to pick up the pieces and go

God can and will transform society.

on instead of moving out of town. Those that did leave town promptly found their way back. To God's glory, the impact of the church—spiritually, economically and socially—was overwhelmingly obvious.

A CHURCH THAT BUILDS THE NATION

The mission statement of our ministry is "building the people that build the nation." I believe that a nation can only be as great as its people. The well-being of individual families will produce a virile nation, spiritually and economically. God can and will transform society. In our ministry we celebrate regularly with people who have just purchased new cars or who have built homes. Most of these are people whose families had given up on their ever amounting to anything, and they struggled with low self-esteem until they found deliverance from demonic influence through our ministry. Amazingly, many of them had no prospect whatsoever of making a successful living on their own. Now many of them actually control million-dollar investments. These things have happened because the people were delivered from the destructive powers that I described earlier.

Over the years, I have encouraged Christians in our ministry to become active in politics. This is borne out of a personal conviction that our prayers need a vehicle in order to transform the nation. I have been blessed to pastor people who have had a direct influence on the decision-making machinery of the country. Over the years this has accelerated economic transformation as these believers have governed with a fear of the Lord—as opposed to the average Nigerian politician, whose trademark is embezzlement of public funds. It is not unusual therefore to see governors, senators, county commissioners and other top government officials regularly attending our services.

God is even turning around the fortunes of Nigerians abroad through the ministry that God has blessed us with. Take the story of a young man who was barely surviving in the Netherlands. He chose to serve us while I was ministering in the Netherlands, and he was convinced that as he served and received hands-on ministry from us, God would bless him. Today, he sits at the helm of a multimillion-dollar phone card business. He is now so blessed financially that he insists on paying all my expenses whenever I am ministering in the Netherlands. I have even resorted to avoiding him when I visit the Netherlands so that he doesn't spend so much money on me! He is but one example of Nigerians abroad who are taking frontline positions because of the power of the Word of God.

The School of Deliverance

I strongly believe in the power of prevailing prayer, and I have inculcated this same spirit in Word of Life Bible Church. As stated earlier, we hold a regular school of deliverance, where people under severe demonic attacks are counseled and delivered. This school runs in three-month cycles, and every participant goes through three different classes. Because of the hunger for deliverance among people in this part of the country, the school serves not only the members of our congregation but also the rest of our city. Countless people are delivered from satanic chains and oppression through attendance at our school of deliverance.

Back in 1974, I was traveling by taxi to Sapele, another town in southern Nigeria. A woman traveling in the same taxi began dropping white chalk out the window into the river as we approached bridges. When I asked why she was doing that, she explained that her mother was a mermaid (Mami Wata spirit)

People will always turn from darkness when they see a demonstration of the power of God with their own eyes.

and lived in the water. This act, she said, would appease the spirits that ruled over the water. I asked the driver to stop the vehicle so that she could get out and go to the water, where her mother was. I then took advantage of her hesitation by sharing Christ with her. She immediately gave her life to the Lord and was completely delivered.

These demonic powers cause great deception. One lady boasted that she was a queen in the spirit world. Another told of how she had received numerous material gifts from her benefactor from the river (for this reason she had chosen to live by the bank of the river). Because of the strength of this deception of reward and protection, some of these people who are oppressed enjoy certain benefits from their oppression—until they somehow fall out of line with their wicked master. It is only then that they willingly seek deliverance.

Greater Power

The powers of darkness in Nigeria are so strong that many people need to see the miraculous in order to believe that there is a power greater than that which they already possess. This became clear to me early in my ministry through an incident that occurred in 1973, when I was a Bible college student in Benin City. Fellow students and I were out doing street evangelism when I came to a home where I heard people crying. I soon learned that a child of the family had just died. My immediate thought was that God could raise the child from the dead, and I told the family so. Not surprisingly, they looked at me as if I were crazy. I then remembered what Jesus had done, so I asked everyone to leave the room (see Mark 5:35-43). I rebuked the spirit of death and called the life of the child back to her body. To the great amazement of all, the child came back to life! The result of this miracle was that her mother, who had previously been a staunch worshiper of Olokun (another name for Mami Wata), gave her life to the Lord and joined the church. Over the years I have seen this happen with great regularity. People will always turn from darkness when they see a demonstration of the power of God with their own eyes (see Luke 7:22).

CONFRONTATION WITH THE RULING SPIRITS

The prophet Daniel experienced the hindrance of ruling spirits. The manifestation of God's presence in the land had stalled for a period of time—imagine all of the oppression that would have gone on as the ruling spirits gained control of the land! The prince of Persia was a spirit who had control over the region. God wanted to visit His people in order to liberate them from the shackles of the enemy, bring them prosperity and give them an identity. His visitation finally came because the children of Israel had cried before Him and their cries had attracted His attention. The prince of Persia knew his days were numbered as he saw his hold over the people of the land being slowly but surely broken. He was not about to take that lightly. Daniel 10:13 (*NIV*) records:

> But the prince of the Persian kingdom resisted me twenty-one days. Then Michael, one of the chief princes, came to help me, because I was detained there with the king of Persia.

In like manner, God's visitation on the nation of Nigeria, and more specifically the southern part of Nigeria, has been challenged in no small measure by the ruling princes. Confrontation is commonplace.

Example 1

The ruling powers send their agents to our deliverance and revival meetings meetings with the sole aim of weakening the services. An example of this happened one night during the opening service of a revival meeting in a small town called Enerhen. The service was jam-packed with people; but as I preached, a man who was standing rather rigidly at the back of the auditorium caught my attention. He had a strange-looking piece of cloth in his hand, which he waved around him in a peculiar manner. I continued to preach anyway. I finished the service and went home.

I was later told what had happened. This man, an agent of the ruling spirits of that community, had been sent to disrupt the meeting. He became restless when he saw a ring of fire burning around him; at first he became paralyzed with fear and could not move. Then he began to wave the cloth in an attempt to put out the fire. People around him did not see this fire, but apparently, he was having a hard time with it! Later, he confessed what was happening and asked some Christians from the meeting to escort him home. He surrendered all his charms because of the mighty demonstration of the power of God that he had witnessed. I praise God that today he is child of God and serves in our church as an usher.

Example 2

On another occasion, we had organized a weekend crusade in the then very small town of Mosogar. On Sunday morning, I was in a car on the way to the church in the company of a brother who was driving when, through the rearview mirror, I saw a woman behind us standing in the narrow forest road. I noticed that this woman had a leaf in her hand. She was talking to the leaf and pointing it toward our tire marks. I immediately told the brother to stop the car. I got out and confronted the woman. I began to speak in tongues, and then I said, "In Jesus' name I nullify all your works; I destroy your powers." She promptly scampered away like a dog with its tail between its legs.

Evidently she was an agent of one of the ruling powers in that area. Her assignment had been to obstruct my mission in that area by causing the vehicle in which I was riding to have an accident.

The spirits got wind of the fact that I had come to shake things up and that I had been sent by Jesus to uproot their evil works. I soon came to learn that prior to my visiting this town, many godly ministers had experienced fatal accidents as a direct result of this woman's nefarious activities. Today there are numerous thriving churches in that region.

Example 3

Because the ruling powers perceived that I was making progress with the peace-making initiatives during the wars in the city of Warri and because of the spiritual destruction of demonic altars, my ministry and I became prime targets for hostility. The enemy openly confronted us on both spiritual and physical fronts.

Looking back, I see a parallel with Nehemiah, who, in seeking to rebuild the broken walls, was faced with opposition—both spiritual and physical. Sanballat was the leading opponent to the rebuilding of God's house and people.

> When word came to Sanballat, Tobiah, Geshem the Arab and the rest of our enemies that I had rebuilt the wall and not a gap was left in it—though up to that time I had not set the doors in the gates—Sanballat and Geshem sent me this message: "Come, let us meet together in one of the villages on the plain of Ono." But they were scheming to harm me (Neh. 6:1-2, *NIV*).

As in the days of Nehemiah, there exist Sanballats today. They are the people whom the devil has anointed to oppose the ministry of the Word of God.

I was informed about a woman, an agent of the ruling spirits, who had been assigned to attack my work and ministry. She obtained a copy of my photograph and buried it in the ground. She performed juju (spells and enchantments) over it with the express intention of causing me bodily harm. Unfortunately for her, the plan backfired and she became the recipient of her own evil intentions. She went mad!

GOD'S PREVAILING POWER

It is the Lord who fights my battles. Read what Solomon says in Proverbs 26:2 (*NIV*):

> Like a fluttering sparrow or a darting swallow, an undeserved curse does not come to rest.

No doubt, demonic ruling powers are real, but the power of God is much more so. This means that in our generation we will be witnesses to the transforming power of the Spirit of God. With the winds of revival blowing stronger every day, the Church of Jesus Christ is continually gaining ground from the enemy of our souls; we are becoming more and more dominant. Glory to the Lord! For indeed, as it is written, "The kingdoms of this world have become the kingdoms of our Lord and of His Christ, and He shall reign forever and ever!" (Rev. 11:15). To this I say a resounding amen!

CHAPTER FIVE

PRAYING TO SEE GOD'S PROMISES

Joe Olaiya

Joe Olaiya has a calling to train and disciple individuals in order that they might fulfill their calling and divinely inspired purpose. He does this primarily through Living Faith Foundation, a ministry founded by him and headquartered in the largely Islamic Kaduna State in northern Nigeria.

Living Faith Foundation, which began as an evangelistic training mission to prepare men for power evangelism, has today established strong branches in the northwestern, north central and northeastern parts of Nigeria. In addition to establishing the churches in the North, Living Faith Foundation has planted a church in Lagos to establish the ministry's base in the southern part of the country.

Preaching the gospel of the Kingdom with a demonstration of signs and wonders has become the hallmark of Living Faith Foundation. Prayer, deliverance and prophetic ministries are also key emphases. Alheri Prayer Camp, housed on 50 acres of land, is the prayer base of Living Faith Foundation, where daily 24-hour prayer is ongoing.

Olaiya is the author of numerous books.

Joe has been happily married to Florence, his wife and helpmate for over 20 years. Together they have three sons and a daughter. He can be reached by e-mail at lffharpazo@yahoo.com.

The gospel first came into Nigeria through European and American missionaries, most of whom were mainstream evangelicals. They believed the Bible and they shared the true plan of salvation, but they had little concept of the power of the Holy Spirit that Jesus had promised in Acts 1:8. Their primary objective was to communicate the basics of the gospel to the Africans.

This traditional missionary approach worked to a degree, partly because the gospel they brought came as part of a larger package of Western education, medicine and civilization. However, the impact of this limited version of the gospel upon African lives was more shallow than the missionaries had intended. It may have "Christianized" and "civilized" our fathers, but it could provide no viable alternative to the supernatural powers and benefits that the gods of their ancestors offered. So while our fathers received Christianity with all the civilizing benefits that came with it, they also carefully preserved their links with their pagan gods, either openly or secretly, so that in times of need they would not be without help. Such spiritual harlotry, as the Old Testament prophets would term it, was the practice of many who admired Christianity for its beauty and blessings but who still looked to their indigenous gods to meet their immediate needs for supernatural power.

The advent of power evangelism as the main vehicle for soul winning and salvation in Africa came later, with the historic transition from the traditional gospel message to the Pentecostal gospel message. The Pentecostal message came into Nigeria at the end of the nineteenth century and the beginning of the twentieth century through the southwestern city of Lagos. The Faith Tabernacle from America made an entrance and gained some converts, while in the eastern part of the country, the Assemblies of God made headway. And due to their loyalty to Britain, the Pentecostal converts of the southwest invited the United Kingdom-based Apostolic Church of Christ to come to Nigeria. They helped introduce the permanent power base for effective evangelism. Through the filling of the Holy Spirit, Nigerian believers now had the necessary power to turn completely from idolatry, to protect themselves from the wrath of the demon gods and even to rescue others from the bondage of the spirits of darkness that had for so long held them in terror and torment.

REVIVAL IN NIGERIA

The revival that hit Nigeria came in phases. First of all, it began with the outpouring of signs and wonders, which, as I have mentioned, had a devastating impact on idolatry in the entire southwest of Nigeria. This came through the ministry of leaders like apostle Babalola, who brought the Apostolic Church from the United Kingdom and founded Christ Apostolic Church. Apostle Orekoya is another Nigerian pioneer who boldly confronted the powers of darkness in order to set the captives free.

At this time a significant seed was being planted by the evangelicals among the literate younger generation through educational institutions. Although this seed lacked knowledge of the Holy Spirit, it was later transformed, merging with the power gospel, and became a vehicle through which true revival would engulf the nation.

Literature soon became a powerful tool in the hands of the Holy Spirit, channeling the fire that would breed the next generation of full-gospel ministers in the nation. Testimonies, teachings, sermons and stories of miracles, signs and wonders were documented in various media such as literature, audiocassettes, videocassettes, radio and television. This greatly helped spread true revival fires across the nation.

Revival's Early Emphases

The emphases of this Holy Spirit revival came through the younger generation, in waves. First came an emphasis on simple repentance. The next wave was healing. Then came the holiness revival, followed closely by an overwhelming focus on prosperity. The pains of abject poverty, which had plagued numerous Nigerians, made the prosperity message extremely attractive. Unfortunately, what God had taught us about repentance and holiness was put to one side because of the desire for material things. Some even concluded that if they had enough faith, they could willfully continue in sin because grace would abound.

The easy blend of faith, grace, liberty and prosperity, which focused on "the abundant life," produced a Church that craved affluence and luxury, that was clothed in pride and that was shamefully bound in sin. Many preachers had abandoned the message of the joy of salvation and the transformation from sin to righteousness for the lure of the comforts that money could bring. The result was devastating. It produced a monstrous Church that on the one hand was Christ believing and tongue talking, but on the other hand was sin bound, adorned in pride and arrogance and spiritually destitute, heading down the slippery slope of error. No wonder that some Western critics would say that the African Church was a mile wide and only an inch deep.

A New Day

Things are now changing in Nigeria. We have entered a new day for the gospel. In the midst of this growing display of gospel abuse in the churches was born a new generation of firebrands—sincere, sin-hating, devil-dislodging Christian leaders. They did not turn against the gospel of prosperity, but they became determined to balance it with the teachings of the whole gospel message. They began to restore the biblical truths of repentance and holiness without compromising the message of salvation and prosperity.

THE AUTHORITY OF THE SPIRITUAL

Because of our pagan background, we Nigerians have an inbred insight into the authority that the spiritual has over the natural. The overwhelming influence of spiritual power is well understood in all aspects of life. Herein lies the need for Nigerians to seek spiritual intervention in virtually everything that we do. Win a battle in the spiritual, and you are sure to win it in the physical. The apostle Paul says, "We do not look at the things which are seen, but at the things which are not seen. For the things which are seen are temporary, but the things which are not seen are eternal" (2 Cor. 4:18).

With this in mind, we can comprehend the story of David and Goliath. From a human perspective, the overwhelmingly stronger giant was better equipped and trained for war. However, he lost the battle to an untrained, poorly armed shepherd boy. The reason that this happened lies in the fact that

David had spiritually prepared himself for the battle. If you pay close attention to the words of both Goliath and David, you will discover that the final anchor of each one consisted of their contact with the supernatural. Their war was fought first in the spiritual realm and then in the physical realm.

The giant drew strength from his gods: "And the Philistine cursed David by his gods" (1 Sam. 17:43). David responded by declaring that he fought "in the name of the LORD of hosts, the God of the armies of Israel" (1 Sam. 17:45). Once these forces were engaged in the spiritual world, the outcome in the natural world became a foregone conclusion.

CONFRONTATION WITH THE INVISIBLE

The story of David brings to mind my encounter with a man who had made a pact with demons. I had just graduated from college, and I was bubbling with a zeal for work and a passion for my profession. I was a civil engineer with the ambition to become a big-time contractor in the future. This goal prompted me to work with large and established contractors. As a Christian, I cherished integrity and detested dishonest gain. Faithfulness to my employers and fairness to my subordinates were my policy.

Soon I stumbled upon information about a particular subcontractor who had a history of being overpaid. Since I had no intention of continuing this dishonest practice, I contacted the relevant parties in order to work out fair remuneration for their current job, taking into consideration the payments they had already received. Their first reaction was to offer me money to overlook the previous payments and to just move on. When I decisively declined their offer of a bribe, they marked me as their enemy, and they began to employ all sorts of devices ranging from intimidation and blackmail to enchantment and witchcraft.

The chauffeur assigned to me was the first to alert me of this turn of events. Since he himself was a man who was fairly knowledgeable of the powers of darkness and who hated injustice, he kindly offered to introduce me to some spiritual power brokers, or mediums, who could provide me with spiritual security and support. I graciously declined his offer and assured him that I was well fortified spiritually.

Shortly thereafter, I had my first confrontation. Very early one morning as I was going into my office at the construction site, the subcontractor accosted me with some charms and amulets in an attempt to place a spell on me. He recited incantations and pronounced curses, but I refused to pay any attention. I then told my boss about this spiritual assault, but I assured him that no harm would come to me through it.

The Showdown

The second confrontation occurred about a month later when this man realized that I was not going to yield to his wishes. His new attack was more vicious than the first, so I decided that it was time to respond and to ensure that he did not believe that his threatened spells would affect me. The Holy Spirit prepared me for this assault, much as He had prepared David: by giving me practice in the art of spiritual warfare. I knew that I had to respond to the attacks from a spiritual perspective, which my protagonist would understand. My objective was to let him know that the powers he was employing were no match for the power of God, which was available to me. I also let him know that he could choose to continue his attack, but if he did, he would then face the wrath of my God.

Not in the least intimidated, I gave my adversary, the subcontractor, my full name to help in his consultation with the occult practitioners. This gesture demonstrated to him my security and confidence in the Lord of hosts, the source of my strength. I then informed him that I was wrapped in my Father's bosom, whose countenance is like lightning and whose eyes are like a flaming fire (see Dan. 10:6). Anyone attempting to play with fire, as my adversary was doing, was liable to get irreparably burned.

Finally, I told him that he had only seven days in which to display the might of his gods and release his demonic hordes against me. I assured him that if he failed in this attempt, I would invoke the judgment of God and that God's wrath would be let loose on him. With this, he began to realize that I was willing to withstand even his greatest onslaught: death. Knowing this, I then said to him, "He who swallowed death and refused to die lives on the inside of me. Even though you send death as your missile, I will swallow it and yet live."

> *Our battle was not in the visible world with law, contracts, courts and financial dealings; it was in the invisible world, just as the struggle between David and Goliath had been.*

At this point, it became clear to him and to everyone else that the battle lines were drawn. This did two things: First, it served as a notice to the kingdom of darkness that I had real supernatural power on my side, which caused tremendous fear to arise in my assailant. Second, it caused those who were observing the power encounter to begin to wonder about the outcome of the battle. Whose power would turn out to be greater?

The Witch Doctor's Defeat

About five days later, the subcontractor went to my boss to ask him to intercede on his behalf and make peace with me. He later came to me personally to apologize and announce his withdrawal from the spiritual battle. It was then that I discovered that he himself was a witch doctor to whom other people went for help. Moreover, he came from a family traditionally known as the chief custodians of the powers of darkness in their region. As a result of his defeat, the subcontractor could not continue his dishonest practices.

Our battle was not in the visible world with laws, contracts, courts and financial dealings; it was in the invisible world, just as the struggle between David and Goliath had been. The point I am making by telling these stories is that the spiritual has authority over the physical.

TERRITORIAL SPIRITS

Practically every territory and people group in Africa is policed by certain principalities of darkness. Often when we would hold a revival meeting, these evil spirits would fight back and raise stiff opposition. When we were careless, they could cause us to suffer numerous spiritual casualties. The prince of Sokoto is one such territorial spirit that has opposed us.

The Prince of Sokoto

The Lord assigned me to minister in Sokoto, the principal city of Islam in Nigeria, for 16 years. The opposition to evangelism was stiff: Christians were suppressed, and evangelism was viewed as an assault and an offense and was greeted with stiff penalties. Those of us who decided to embrace the freedoms of speech and worship, which are guaranteed in the nation's constitution, were treated as outlaws and literally targeted for elimination. In the midst of all this, the call to invade the land and raise an army for ministry was confirmed by the Lord. This strengthened my conviction to carry on.

I remember well the spiritual opposition the first church we opened in Sokoto faced. We had been holding services for a few weeks, but it was was extremely difficult to preach in those services. In spite of much prayer, the heavens over the newly built church seemed completely closed. Preaching to the same kind of people anywhere else seemed inspired, anointed and exciting. What, then, could be the reason for my struggle each time I attempted to preach at this location? I began to seek the Lord for a solution. I agonized in my spirit like one who was climbing up a steep hill. Then, one night while I slept, the revelation came in a dream. I saw myself standing on the platform in the new church building, as if preparing to preach a sermon. Suddenly, an enormous black man came from behind me. He appeared to be 12 feet tall, and he grasped my neck, making it difficult for me to speak. He demanded to know why I had come to take his land and who had given me the authority to intrude and preach this forbidden message here.

Then I woke up, and I began to meditate on the revelation. God immediately showed me that I had just been face-to-face with the territorial spirit whom Satan had assigned to keep the town of Sokoto in darkness. I knew that I needed to pray and fast intensely and then challenge that wicked spirit to direct spiritual warfare. I did so. It was intense, but after three days and three nights, the battle had been fought and won. The following Sunday, the heavens were open—more open than they had never been before. From that day on, God began to perform miracles, and the church grew.

The Prince of Persia

These encounters with ruling powers readily bring to mind biblical scenes such as Daniel's prayer, which is recorded in Daniel 9 and 10. Who is this prince of Persia that withstood, resisted and opposed the angel Gabriel for 21 days, delaying Gabriel's arrival to deliver the answer to Daniel's prayers (see Dan. 10:13)? Who is this prince of Greece (see Dan. 10:20)? Clearly, according to the Scriptures, these were ruling territorial spirits who sought to hinder the plans and purposes of God.

THE PRINCESS

It could be possible that some who read this book have concluded that the idea of territorial spirits is simply a figment of our imagination. A frequent comment from Westerners is that Africans tend to be overly superstitious, but here's a reality check. Allow me to tell you a story that will show how powerful these spirits can be. I do not do this to glorify evil spirits; rather, I do it because our spiritual warfare will be informed and successful to the same degree that we understand our enemy.

A Vision of the Princess

At one point, I had scheduled soul-winning outreaches in two neighboring communities, Zuru and Tungan Magajiya. Everything was in place; but before we left home for the campaign, my wife had a vision in which she saw a princess who was complaining bitterly that we were coming to her land to remove her children without obtaining proper permission from her. The princess threatened to get back at us. I made the mistake of nonchalantly responding to this revelation. Instead of doing battle against the princess in spiritual warfare, I foolishly told my wife not to worry about her. I claimed that the princess was powerless to do anything and that we should put the matter aside.

A Powerful Outreach

The night before the outreach started, our team spent the evening praying in a church on the hillside. After midnight, I left the prayer meeting to go up on the hilltop in order to be alone with God. While I was there, the heavens opened and the Lord told me that from then on, the blind would see, the lame would walk, the deaf would hear, and many miracles would highlight our meetings. Upon receiving this word, I rejoined the prayer warriors and brought the meeting to a close.

True to this word, the blind saw, the deaf heard, and many others were healed of their diseases. In addition, demons were cast out. These miracles naturally caused a lot of people to be saved. The news of God's blessing spread far and wide; and by the time we reached the next community, the ground was even more fertile. On the last day of the outreach, I preached a message entitled "Eternity: Preparing to Meet God." So great was the response to the altar call and so exciting was the night of ministry that people did not want to leave because of the joy that permeated the atmosphere.

The Revenge of the Princess

Now, how does the princess who was revealed to my wife as the territorial spirit fit in? Little did we realize that we had infuriated the wicked princess as a result of the loss her kingdom had suffered.

The team had traveled to the outreach in two buses. On the return journey, about 25 miles from our home I drove past the two buses. I had hardly settled in after arriving home when I received the shocking news: The princess had struck! She had kept her promise to strike back! One of the buses had been involved in a collision; and in that tragic accident, we lost one lady, two men and two children!

The pain and distress that came over me kept me from eating for seven days. Worse still was the fact that I had no answer to the barrage of questions that followed. Were these casualties due to my carelessness? What if I had taken seriously the threat of the princess in my wife's dream and fought her rather than disregard her threat? The difficult answers did not come immediately.

A Casuality-Free Outreach

Our next evangelistic outreach was already scheduled to occur three months later. I thought about putting it off; but not wanting to give in to the enemy's assaults, I decided against that course of action. We held the outreach, and this time there were no casualties. In fact, God had promised that we would not have any more casualties.

Some Questions Answered

As time went by, we slowly healed from the pain of our loss, but the questions about the power of our enemy, the devil, remained unanswered—until we began to realize the following:

- The enemy always reacts negatively to soul-winning, healing and deliverance outreaches.
- The enemy will usually look for the weakest links in the team and attempt to strike the team through them.
- The enemy typically becomes more effective if he can send a human agent to infiltrate the camp and work among us.
- Postoutreach prayer guard is as important as pre-outreach prayer assaults in order to provide a shield of protection around the participants.
- We must take spiritual information (such as the revelation to my wife) seriously and act on it wisely.

The Defeat of the Princess

We received the complete answer a year after our loss. After another successful and very fruitful soul-winning campaign, we were having a feast for the new converts. We all were in a festive mood, celebrating the joy of salvation. One of our team members left the campaign ground to go home. Just after she left, she suddenly fell flat on her face. When a passerby helped her up, she staggered and fell again. Someone who was also at the feast recognized her and brought her back for proper attention.

When word about her collapse reached me, I rushed out to investigate the matter. When I asked her what was wrong, she gave me an unexpected but rather interesting answer. She confessed that she was a witch. I promptly asked whether or not she knew what she was saying. She replied in the affirmative that she truly was a witch. When I demanded to know how she had received her powers, she replied that she had been initiated as a child over 40 years earlier.

This witch went on to confess that she had aligned herself with the powers of darkness to penetrate the team and to cause the bus accident. She had been the opening for the enemy. This woman had succeeded in throwing us off the scent by appearing more emotionally distraught than anyone else after the accident. She had even fooled me by throwing an emotional fit and pounding me with her fists, demanding that I bring back to life one of the people who had died.

She further spoke of some other evil deeds she had put in motion in the lives of various people, especially those who had trusted her and who were the closest to her. At this point, I demanded that the arresting officer prosecute her to the full extent of the law. This was done, but it proved to be only the beginning of her troubles. Restlessness, insomnia, a lack of physical coordination and public displays of shameful indecent exposure all became regular parts of her life.

I sent for people who had been placed under her spell, and I put them on a fast in order to break the powers of darkness over their lives. The results were amazing! We saw immediate reversals of the harm done to these people. Their lives progressed, their fortunes were restored, and they enjoyed God's blessings. The princess may have gained a temporary victory, but ultimately she suffered a permanent loss!

THE RULERS OF KAFANCHAN

The next gospel campaign was slated for Kafanchan, a prominent city in Kaduna State in northern Nigeria. The city had been fully prepared for the campaign, and the advance team was already on site doing final preparations. Even though I was tired, the Holy Spirit prompted me to go to Kafanchan a day earlier than I had planned.

Within three hours of arriving in Kafanchan, I had a clear vision in which I was taken down into the meeting place of the rulers of darkness of the region. I was brought into their gathering from the rear so that they did not know that I was there. They all sat down, except for their leader, who was addressing them. This leader, the territorial spirit over the area, stood upright like a man but looked like a beast, and he wore traditional Nigerian attire. He was fuming with rage and said with intensity, "He is coming again to take our children, and he has not asked our permission. This time, he will not succeed; neither will he go free." At this point, I was led out of their meeting, but later I directly received from the Holy Spirit their detailed plan of operation as well as the battle plan for how I was to respond.

Strife and Division

The Holy Spirit showed me that they had plotted to work through my campaign operations manager, a man who was somewhat temperamental. He had been known to generate strife among the team, thus opening the doors for demonic attacks to be launched against us. The powers of darkness hoped to work through this disunity and bitterness. Their stated coup de grâce would be to cause a fatal accident on our return journey, much as the princess had done.

I immediately called the senior pastors who were with me and warned them of the possibility of strife. Shortly after, they left for the campaign venue, where they would have had the shock of their lives, except for the fact that they had been prepared by my warning. When they arrived, they found the operations manager irrationally enraged with them over some issues involving money. In addition, the manager even abandoned the work of setting up the stage and equipment. This turn of events was a considerable setback for us.

Remembering my warning, the senior pastors rolled up their sleeves and took over the preparations for the campaign, while I immediately began a personal fast. I continued in prayer warfare up until the moment that the meeting was scheduled to start. The Holy Spirit specifically revealed to me that certain hoodlums, taking full advantage of the generated strife, would come to the meeting to disrupt the move of the Holy Spirit. However, they would be dispersed by an apostolic declaration that the Holy Spirit instructed me to make as soon as I took the stage.

An Apostolic Declaration
Unfortunately, when I arrived at the campaign site, I was so upset by the issue of the unfinished preparation that I could not concentrate. The hoodlums were there; but by the time I got up to preach, I had forgotten about making the declaration, and I went ahead and preached without it. The results were only average—with very few miracles and a mediocre response to the salvation call. Afterward, I pondered what might have gone amiss, and I suddenly remembered that I had neglected to speak the declaration as the Holy Spirit had instructed me to do.

The next day, the hoodlums were again at the service. But this time I made the following declaration: "Let God arise, let His enemies be scattered; let those also who hate Him flee before Him. As smoke is driven away, so drive them away; as wax melts before the fire, so let the wicked perish at the presence of God" (Ps. 68:1-2). As I made this declaration, there was in the spirit realm an explosion that broke through every barrier and immediately created an open heaven.

The results of the ministry that night were wonderful. Miracles were graciously released and blessings were poured out. The spirit of salvation was mightily at work and many souls were snatched from hell. The final day was even more explosive. So great were the results and the flow of divine power that men and women were held completely spellbound until 1:00 A.M.

Not only was the campaign a tremendous success, but also the influence of strife was completely disarmed. The operations manager suddenly repented of his ungodly attitude. We had joy all the way back home and did not suffer any of the casualties that the enemy had plotted.

CATALYSTS OF CHURCH GROWTH IN NORTHERN NIGERIA

In the midst of the strong spiritual opposition that our churches in the Muslim-controlled area of northern Nigeria face, God proves Himself infinitely stronger and causes the churches to grow. We believers in the North have chosen to partner with God. What are the principal human factors promoting the churches' growth? I think there are four:

1. The evangelism factor—the practical pursuit of soul winning with passion

2. The holiness factor—an emphasis on righteousness and holiness in word and deed
3. The prayer factor—a commitment to warfare prayer and praying with results
4. The miracle and deliverance factor—the demonstration of the power of God in diverse human situations

Let me stress the enormous power generated by fasting and prayer, especially in conjunction with spiritual warfare. Our understanding of the spiritual opposition we face, as well as our

> *The spiritual landscape of any nation will not change appreciably until we involve ourselves in intensive, fervent intercession and fasting for the land.*

authority over all kinds of spirits, is significantly greater when accompanied by prayer and fasting. I am convinced that the spiritual landscape of any nation will not change appreciably until we involve ourselves in intensive, fervent intercession and fasting for the land.

Much of the breakthrough in northern Nigeria has come through this kind of intercession. The spirit of the bondswoman, which is the ruling principality of Islam, is known to be very oppressive and bloodthirsty. It is also characterized by hatred and violence. Engaging such a principality, especially when political power is vested in its agents, requires wisdom coupled with the power of prayer.

Today, by the grace of God, churches are growing in the land despite several assaults on Christian lives and church properties. The Lord is making room for His Church. Wisdom dictates that we cannot give detailed accounts of some of the things we have faced in these relatively antigospel, hostile zones. Suffice it to say, however, in all these the Church is marching on and the gates of hell are falling.

REVIVAL FIRES

The current revival in the nation of Nigeria comes in fulfillment of the promise of God to raise up a mighty army that will take the gospel far beyond the boundaries of our nation. The only way we can maintain the momentum is to keep in step with God's divine drumbeat. We must maintain our focus. We must not allow other passions to replace our passion for souls. The tombstones of many past revivals bear the epitaph "They lost their passion for God." When the love of money, the pride of life or other such pursuits overshadow our zeal for the Lord's work, we can begin to love the blessings more than the blesser. Many revivals die a premature death: When the life of God in them has dissipated, they cease to be living organisms and instead become great human organizations. Life then is replaced with laws and legacies, and spiritual power is replaced with financial power.

We must not let this fire of revival die! We must maintain our focus until the entire world is engulfed with the flames that now consume our nation. The torch must be passed on to the next generation. We who are leaders today must not fail to disciple the next generation in the spiritual fervor that is required to continue His work. The sacrifice? Dedication and zeal, which must not be sidelined for comfort, luxury or pleasure. We have this great treasure in earthen vessels! God makes

His power available to us, but it is our responsibility to pray until we see God's promises fulfilled!

CHAPTER SIX

MISSIONARY TO LONDON

Sola Fola-Alade

Sola Fola-Alade was trained and practiced as a medical doctor. He now pastors Trinity Chapel (a part of the Redeemed Christian Church of God) in Stratford, England, a growing and dynamic church that he and five others started in 1996.

He is the author of two popular books, Discover Your Hidden Treasures *and* So, Who Do You Really Think You Are? *These books have attracted the attention of both Christian and secular media alike, such as BBC WM, Premier Radio and* West Africa *magazine.*

Dr. Fola-Alade is passionate about healing the wounded person from within and about preparing Christians as leaders in the workplace.

He was trained at International Bible Institute of London, Kensington Temple, and later went on to earn an MBA at East London Business School.

Sola is happily married to Abimbola, and they have two sons, Toni and Tola.

It was about 5:15 A.M., and the captain aboard the British Airways flight rudely interrupted my already fitful sleep as he announced that we would be landing at London's Heathrow airport within the next 15 minutes. The temperature, he said, would be a chilly 45 degrees. Compared with the balmy 90-degree weather in Lagos, Nigeria, this seemed frighteningly cold.

I could feel a dry lump in my throat as we approached our destination. I was feeling quite worn out, as I had hardly gotten a wink of sleep. How, in fact, could I sleep aboard a flight to destiny? Considering the reality that I had just said good night to the familiar and the comfortable and was now awakening to a new day in a strange land in which I did not know what to expect, I began to identify very closely with the story of Abram and his call to a foreign land (see Gen. 12:1-3). This wasn't by any means unfamiliar territory, as I had already been in London on numerous occasions. From about the age of seven, my family and I had visited the United Kingdom quite regularly on vacation. In fact, I had been in the United Kingdom just a month earlier on vacation, but somehow this trip was different.

MISSION TO LONDON

I had left the comfort of my family and of my native land, Nigeria, in response to an overwhelming sense that God was calling me to move to London to be a long-term missionary. Somehow, this knowledge made the trip a little different from all the previous trips I had made. Now there was a sense of finality to the journey. Now there was an overwhelming sense of destiny as I headed into the unknown. This wasn't just another vacation from which I would return in a few short weeks.

I had left behind a blossoming career as a medical doctor and a thriving design, print and publishing business, as well as the comfort of home and the support of my family, in obedience to God—although against my father's wishes—in order to fulfill a calling to serve the nations. From where I was sitting, I could not avoid the feelings of anxiety that threatened to overwhelm me. I was clueless as to what tomorrow might bring—not to mention the next 12 months. The only thing I was certain of was that I had been asked to leave all my lucrative business and career pursuits in order to serve as an assistant pastor, under Pastor Agu Irukwu of Jesus House, London, the flagship church of the Redeemed Christian Church of God (RCCG) in the United Kingdom.

At that time there were approximately 10 branch churches of the RCCG in the United Kingdom (now there are about 100). Given the RCCG's goal of establishing a church within convenient walking distance in every neighborhood, I was informed a few days before leaving for the United Kingdom that there had been a slight change of plans. I was now no longer assigned to assist pastor Agu at Jesus House; instead, I was going to be sent out with a team of five other people and £250 (approximately $416) to plant a new church in the East End of London.

The lump in my throat doubled in size and threatened to push its way through my neck as I contemplated the recent turn of events. As our plane began to make its final descent, I, frankly, felt afraid and very alone. The only thing that brought any measure of relief was recalling the promise God had spoken to me as I left my home and country. It was the same promise He had spoken to Abraham in Ur of the Chaldeans generations earlier:

> The LORD had said to Abram: "Get out of your country, from your family and from your father's house, to a land that I will show you. I will make you a great nation; I will bless you and make your name great" (Gen. 12:1-3).

Like it or not, the die was cast. It was all or nothing from here on!

HIDDEN TREASURES

Slowly but surely I began to adjust to life in London. It seems like only yesterday, but one evening, shortly after my arrival in London, a friend met me at the Stratford train station to take me on a tour around the borough of Newham so that I could become more familiar with our prospective mission field. With six people on our team and £250 in the bank, it was time to embark on the project of planting a church in London's East End, even though I had barely spent a month with Pastor Agu at Jesus House.

From my vantage point, the future looked as bleak as the station. The station was dilapidated and the surrounding area was dirty and unkempt. This, together with a small bank balance, did little to buoy my spirits. As if that were not a sufficient challenge for a green pastor, two of the six people who had been assigned to form my core team were unemployed and another two were students. The gentleman who took me on the leisurely drive around the borough was my future assistant pastor. Although he was a qualified accountant with an MBA, he had been unemployed for a year and had to make ends meet by driving a minicab. His lovely wife was expecting a baby in a couple of months. The £250 just seemed to get smaller and smaller. To top things off, two weeks after our drive around Newham, my friend's car was impounded by the police and turned into scrap. It had been deemed a hazard because it was releasing toxic emissions into the environment.

On that first day in our new mission field, I learned that the borough of Newham was the second poorest borough in all of London with an unemployment rate 2.9 times the national average. The academic performance of the schools was rated the worst in the country.

My first reaction was an inward desire to turn back. This was not my idea of a suitable place to start what I hoped would be a thriving church. As I looked at the situation before me—the people on the streets and the dismal life ahead—I began to wonder if it might be time to resume my lucrative career as a neurosurgeon. But while I pondered this extremely attractive proposition, I heard a clear voice in my spirit saying, *You have this treasure in earthen vessels.*

Later that day, I lay down to meditate on those words. I felt the Spirit of God saying to me that He had brought me to a very wealthy place. A wealthy place? The borough of Newham? The city of Stratford? Looking around me, I naturally found that idea rather difficult to comprehend.

Then I was reminded that God does not see as people see. Humans judge the outward appearance, but God judges the heart. I also remembered that God, who brings life out of death, uses "things despised by the world . . . to bring to nothing what the world considers important" (1 Cor. 1:28, *NLT*). I recalled a profound saying I had heard:

The wealthiest place in the world is not the gold mines of Ghana, nor the diamond mines of South Africa nor even the oil fields of Kuwait. The wealthiest place in the world is the graveyard.

The graveyard is the place where many undiscovered talents, unfulfilled dreams, untapped treasures and unrealized wealth lay buried. Both millionaires and missionaries who lived and died in relative obscurity lay buried there. Potential prime ministers and would-be world-renowned preachers lay there, many of whom died as paupers. It was this thought that ignited a vision in me for Stratford and its surrounding areas, motivating me to fulfill my mission to discover God's hidden treasures.

Now, seven years later, I have witnessed the miracle of a church that began with six people becoming a church of just under 700 people, with an annual income of over a half million pounds (approximately $831,510)—and it continues to grow by leaps and bounds. What became of the unemployed accountant turned minicab driver? He became a business consultant with one of the Fortune 500 companies and now runs his own consulting firm. By the grace and power of God, I have seen hordes of people walk through the doors of the church and receive fresh vision for their lives and families.

SMALL BEGINNINGS

It is often said, "A journey of a thousand miles begins with one step." Indeed, our first step toward planting a great church was a small and seemingly insignificant one.

I remember well the first service we held. There were no flyers announcing the grand opening and no large edifice built to hold thousands. We began services in an inauspicious living room with a prayer meeting attended by six people. As we prayed, I thought to myself, *We must really be crazy to think that we can build a church of any significance this way.* As we continued to pray, however, I saw a picture in my heart of a little baby wearing an oversized Abraham Lincoln-type top hat. The picture seemed to be a message from God reminding me not to despise small beginnings. I felt that the picture was the Lord's word to us, telling us that our church would grow and prosper but that there would be a price to pay. I further felt that the image of the Lincoln hat was an indication that we would experience many different challenges, just like Abraham Lincoln did, but that we would overcome them and become a church of governmental influence in the United Kingdom during a difficult period in the country's history. And so began the life of Trinity Chapel.

I was extremely excited by the Lincoln-hat revelation. Then I was further encouraged when I heard Pastor Colin Dye of Kensington Temple say, during a lecture at one of my classes at International Bible Institute of London, "Characteristically, every great thing in life starts in a small way." I knew he was speaking to me.

THE AVERAGE CHURCH

I was even more encouraged when a few months after we had started the church, we were seeing an average attendance of 40 people at our services. I had previously heard that the United Kingdom is known as a preacher's graveyard and that the average church membership in England was about 40 people. This is where I made one of my first mistakes: I fell into the trap of becoming quite thankful that God had counted me worthy to pastor an average church in a foreign land. I had become content and rather satisfied with what we were doing and with the number of people attending our services.

Then I listened to a tape by Pastor Matthew Ashimolowo of Kingsway International Christian Centre. Pastor Matthew is a fellow Nigerian who became pastor of Britain's largest church, which has over 8,000 members. In his message, he told the story of how he had first come to the United Kingdom almost two decades earlier and had started a church with just 11 people. For over three years, the church did not grow beyond 40 attendees. He had heard the same story of the 40 people average that I had heard and was told that he ought to be thankful to have 40 members in his church. But God challenged Pastor Matthew to lift his level of faith. Pastor Matthew knew that he must break the power of the limits that he had placed on himself when he believed that his church could not grow beyond 40 people. And as he began to have faith that God had called him to make a more significant impact on the community, his church began to experience growth.

As I listened to Pastor Matthew's story and observed how God seemed to be using other African pastors, especially Nigerian ones, my faith began to grow. I noticed the tremendous growth that Nigerian missionaries like Agu Irukwu, Albert Odulele, Nims Obunge, Tayo Adeyemi, Paul Jinadu and numerous others were experiencing in the city of London. An even more exciting observation I made was that many of them had left thriving careers and professions just as I had done, and they went on to build some of the largest and most significant churches in the United Kingdom.

I was challenged by God through all this to lift up my eyes and see the possibilities that He had laid out before me. I determined then and there that I would step out in faith and achieve great things for Him. I was no longer satisfied with being average!

THE POWER OF VISION

With renewed determination, I took a personal retreat in a countryside location. I was desperate to hear a word from God outlining the direction for the ministry He had committed into my hands. It was during this time that God began to challenge me as He had challenged Abraham: "Lift your eyes now and look from the place where you are" (Gen. 13:14). I felt God impress upon my heart that the team He had given me to work with and I were much like Gideon in the winepress—timid and frustrated, working like elephants and living like ants. We were constrained by the spirit of poverty as Israel had been impoverished by the Midianites. Our perspective limited us from exercising our rightful authority in the spirit realm (see Judg. 6:1-18). At that time, the large majority of church members were working odd jobs as taxi drivers, mail carriers, train station assistants, nurses aides and supermarket clerks, despite the fact that most of them were professionals: doctors, lawyers, accountants with MBAs, and so on.

This divine encounter marked a turning point in my life and ministry in the United Kingdom. I came back from the retreat with renewed vision and determination. I immediately challenged the congregation to break out of small-minded thinking and gave them the vision to overcome the limitations that they had placed on themselves based on what society dictated they could be. I began to challenge my people to be like Habakkuk and watch to see what God would say to them. I challenged them to "write the vision and make it plain" (Hab. 2:1-2).

BREAKTHROUGH INTO DESTINY

The church members were indeed challenged to seek a greater vision for God's destiny in their lives. They began to break out of small-mindedness and a defeatist mentality. No longer seeing themselves as only deserving low-salaried jobs, they began to apply for and secure white-collar jobs. The church members broke through the invisible glass ceiling as they began working successfully in high-paying jobs throughout the city. Many became bankers, corporate lawyers and information technology

(IT) professionals. Not a few were earning six-figure incomes.

Trinity Chapel went from being a predominantly poor, lower-class blue-collar congregation to a professional, middle-class white-collar church in just a matter of months. It was during this same period that my assistant, who had been driving a taxi-cab even though he was a CPA, landed his job with a Fortune 500 company, as I previously mentioned. Another man who had been working as a parking lot attendant got a job as a consultant with one of Britain's top IT firms. Today he runs his own successful IT and business consultating firm. All of this happened after God persuaded me, in the countryside, to cast His church a challenging vision.

It is not surprising that, while all of this was unfolding, the Lord began to stir up in my heart the need to host an annual conference called the Power of Vision. In this conference we encourage and motivate leaders to seek success in every arena, from government and education to the workplace in general. The guest speakers come from all over the world to challenge the people to envision and achieve great things for God. I felt that the Lord had given me a mandate to develop leaders who would influence society in every stratum.

Since the inception of the Power of Vision conference in July 1999, we have had seasoned leaders from various fields of expertise impact us and stir up our vision for even greater things. Every year we are privileged to have outstanding leaders speak to us, leaders like Pastor Matthew Ashimolowo, whom I have already mentioned; and Pastor Ted Haggard, the senior pastor at New Life Church in Colorado Springs, Colorado, and one of the most influential Christian leaders in the United States. We have also heard a number of influential political leaders from the United Kingdom who are committed Christians, such as Stephen Timms, minister for education under Tony Blair's administration, and Ram Gidoomal, head of Christian Peoples

Alliance (CPA), the only Christian political party in the United Kingdom.

A CHURCH OF INFLUENCE

In light of the vision I had received from God to build a church with governmental influence, we felt that no church can have real influence without empowering its people to get involved in the creation of policy. We were convinced that by entering politics, we could help establish policies that embrace a Christian worldview, that influence the minds of the next generation

No church can have real influence on the government without empowering its people to get involved in the creation of policy.

through education and that change paradigms of secular humanism through the media. We began to watch and pray, while constantly challenging and empowering members of our church to get involved in all these arenas. A couple of people in the church ran for the office of councillor in their local boroughs. Our entire church played a significant role in the campaign that saw Alan Craig of CPA elected as the first Christian councillor in the Labor Party stronghold of the borough of Newham, where our church is located.

Trinity Chapel has also seen some of its members take up strategic and influential positions in the workplace in various industries such as financial services, IT consulting, education and so on. One of our most poignant stories is that of the head of our children's church, Mrs. Moji Omole, who is a teacher in a government school in the borough of Newham. There she was recognized by the National Educational Standards Board as having the best, most effective teaching methods in her grade nationwide. She was recommended for recognition by the prime minister of the United Kingdom, Tony Blair. Mrs. Omole is now in the process of setting up a school with Christian values and a biblical foundation for our church. This is quite significant since, as previously stated, the educational performance of schools in Newham is the worst in the country. We anticipate academic improvement for the students we will be privileged to serve. In addition, at least five different couples who are members of the church have started Saturday schools and after-school clubs. Others are in the process of opening preschools to help with the severe shortage of trustworthy, affordable child care in the community.

Another success story concerns a young lady who walked into our church with no real sense of purpose or direction. When I first saw her, I honestly thought she was a hopeless case. But after speaking to her for a few minutes, I felt strongly that God was going to use her very powerfully in the media arena because of her heart, her literary ability and her gift with words. Within a year, she became the managing editor of our vibrant, colorful, monthly news journal. A few months later, she was given a job as a weekly columnist of a national ethnic newspaper called the *African Times*. With her help, connections and expertise, our church conferences and activities have been featured in many local, regional, national and international magazines such as *West Africa*, *Voice*, *New Nation* and various others. She has been extremely instrumental in our church's getting positive media attention. All of this from someone who, just a few short years earlier, had walked into our church without a vision for her future.

We are setting up a crisis-pregnancy center for young girls; the center's services will include legal advice and AIDS counseling. Plans are also in the pipeline to set up a free career advice and debt counseling service. One of the churches that we've planted, Clays Lane Christian Centre, is very involved in providing free Internet services to its community, while another, Gateway Chapel, is involved in business reformation in Kent.

Our music director offers music and voice training to young, undiscovered talent in the community. The church also offers excellent premarital counseling, marriage enhancement training and seminars to empower women, which are currently only open to church members but will, in the near future, be open to the public. These programs are spearheaded and run by my wife, who has left her career as a lawyer to pursue God's dream of impacting the escalating divorce rate both in the church and in the community at large.

ONLY THE BEGINNING

Trinity Chapel is by no means the largest church in London, neither have we reached or come close to achieving our God-breathed vision: to raise up leaders. We can, however, boldly say that God has allowed us to become one of the more significant and influential churches in London. Watch this space! Trinity Chapel is on the move, and it is committed to becoming all that God has designed for it to be. The only limits are the ones we place on ourselves, and like Joseph, we feel that we are poised to become a people of significant influence in a foreign land.

Seven years from the day I arrived in London on my mission into the unknown, I can boldly say that God has been gracious and faithful. The greater testimony is the fact that we have only just begun.

THE LEADERSHIP CENTRE

When Trinity Chapel moved into its new facility, which we call the Leadership Centre, not too long ago, it marked a defining moment. The Leadership Centre is strategically located on a high street and what seems to be a symbolic spiritual gate to the city of Stratford. The building is also located right in the center of an apartment complex with about 900 housing units and some 2,000 residents. We believe that God has given us a mandate to reach that community and that He has also given us the means to do so: We discovered that the chairperson for the housing development is a member of our church. She has made arrangements for our church services to be aired every Sunday on the development's private cable television network. Talk about strategic positioning for influence!

God has given us the desire of our hearts to use our facility for works of service in the community. The city has given us permission to use the Leadership Centre as a conference center. We have begun by regularly holding musical concerts and talent search events for our community.

COMMUNITY TRANSFORMATION

One of the major problems in the city of London, one which has left both the government and police force bewildered, is the problem of troubled youth: teenagers and young adults who are involved in drugs, teenage pregnancy, car theft, vandalism and other such antisocial behavior. The church has plans underway to convert one of the spaces in the Leadership Centre into a drop-in café for young people, along with an Internet and computer training facility. This is intended to help engage these youth in more constructive activities and to keep them off the streets.

CHAPTER SEVEN

THE KINGDOMS OF THIS WORLD

Paul Adefarasin

Paul Adefarasin was born in Lagos, Nigeria. He attended schools in the United Kingdom and Nigeria before pursuing his degree in architecture at the University of Miami.

Following a debilitating drug dependency problem, Paul's call to the ministry came in 1983 as he gave his life to Christ and conquered his addiction. Early in 1990, Paul obeyed a divine summons to go into full-time ministry in Nigeria. He initially worked as a full-time minister at Latter Rain Assembly and The Redeemed Evangelical Mission, Lagos, Nigeria. He then proceeded to Christian Action Faith Ministries, where he was appointed the resident pastor of the London branch of Action Chapel. In December 1993, Paul returned to Nigeria to sort out some travel papers but then was refused a reentry permit to the United Kingdom. This apparent setback sparked off a season of intense prayer, during which House on the Rock and Rock Foundation were birthed. What began as a Friday night prayer meeting with seven people has today become a fast-growing multiracial, multiethnic and multifaceted church with well over 7,000 congregants in the Lagos headquarters. Thirty-five branches of the church have since been birthed in Europe and in Francophone and Anglophone Africa.

Rock Foundation is a ministry committed to restoring hope and heal-ing the hurting in our generation through the identification of and direct ministry to specific needs.

Adefarasin's television program, Something Is About to Happen, *is a favorite among a television audience of well over 30 million viewers spread across Nigeria, parts of West Africa and London.*

Paul is happily married to Ifeanyi, and together they have two lovely children, Hilda Adebola and Alvin Adegboyega.

From one Sunday to the next, Nigerians from all walks of life and from every conceivable economic background flood into the numerous churches spread across the nation. For most, this is not a mere fulfillment of religious obligation; rather, it is the ongoing passionate quest for a personal encounter with an all-powerful God who holds the key to life and destiny. The Scriptures indicate that this is a worthwhile pursuit: "Blessed are those who hunger and thirst for righteousness, for they shall be filled" (Matt. 5:6).

To say that the explosion of Christianity and the number of Bible believing-churches in Nigeria are remarkable would be an understatement. Nigeria, a country too often associated with vices and corruption, has a different side. It is seen by many as the epicenter of one of the greatest moves of God in recent Church history.

A People in Need

In 1958, oil was discovered in southern Nigeria. Before that, Nigeria's economy had been predominantly based on the export of crops such as palm kernels, cocoa and peanuts. With the discovery of crude oil, agriculture took a distant backseat. By the mid 1970s, money—and lots of it—was available everywhere you looked. In almost no time at all, "Spend all you can" became the order of the day. Corruption soon became a way of life among Nigerian leadership, and a nation that had been poised to become one of the richest in the world was suddenly plunged into the murky depths of poverty. With deprivation and oppression growing to an insufferable degree, Nigerians began to look for a real God who could solve real problems. It seemed quite obvious that Nigeria had sunk to new levels of despair. But the story had not yet been fully written.

The Raising of Generals

And God has appointed these in the church: first apostles, second prophets, third teachers, after that miracles, then gifts of healings, helps, administrations, varieties of tongues (1 Cor. 12:28).

In the early 1970s, groups like Scripture Union, Student Christian Movement and Nigerian Fellowship of Evangelical Students introduced the gospel in schools. Many young Nigerians were born again. The real impact of this move, however, would only be appreciated in years to come.

The mid-1970s saw God begin to raise up leaders from the working class. Notable among these was the late Archbishop Benson Idahosa. Archbishop Idahosa is considered by many to be the foremost pioneer of the Pentecostal movement in Nigeria. He was a man of great passion and anointing. Today, many preachers and laypersons owe their conversion to the work of God through his prolific ministry.

Unlike many of the ministers of his time, Benson Idahosa saw the value of education and was himself an educator. The men and women raised in the 1970s were typically very fervent and demonstrated extreme degrees of faith. Even though many did not have the benefit of formal education, they nevertheless gathered great crowds through the raw preaching of the Word with signs following. What might have been lacking in theological study was compensated for with prayer and sheer passion for God.

The downside of many of these ministries, however, was the tendency of some of the followers to embrace a personality cult rather than give primary allegiance to Christ. This may have been due, at least in part, to the inability of the leaders to articulate the biblical principles upon which many of the miracles seen in their ministries were based. Hence personality flaws and unwise excesses were diligently emulated, being mistaken for godly traits. It did not take long before the more educated Nigerians began to associate being born again with poorly mannered, lower-class fanatics who were not able to make anything decent out of their lives. Being born again, it seemed to some, was just a device for copping out of real life.

Then in the late 1970s and early 1980s, many of the young men and women who had been affected by the campus movements began to graduate from college with a hunger and thirst for God. A different kind of leader began to emerge. Men and women with university degrees and from professional working backgrounds began to accept God's call to ministry. Because of their educational background and experience in the workplace, they were able to present the gospel in a way that their worldly counterparts could relate to.

With further economic depression and the partial collapse of several financial institutions, the professional working class was, it appeared, ready to look for God. Leaders like Enoch A. Adeboye, David Oyedepo, William Kumuyi and Mike Okonkwo pioneered moves that saw huge numbers of men and women from professional sectors of society come into the kingdom of God for the first time.

As I saw all of this going on around me, I began to wonder where I would fit.

THE TRANSFORMING POWER OF GOD

I was born to humble but relatively affluent parents. My father was a high court judge and my mother was a nurse. I was privileged to attend some of the best schools and colleges in England and the United States. It was during my time at the University of Miami that I started experimenting with drugs and eventually became thoroughly addicted. Such was the degree of my dependency and sense of hopelessness that on several occasions I came close to taking my own life. I had become an outcast from my family and friends, and the general consensus was that I'd never amount to anything good. For me to graduate and get a job would be in itself an achievement bordering on the miraculous.

And then God touched my life in a way that was as unexpected as it was dramatic. At the time I had scraped the bottom of the barrel, and I had decided to abandon the pursuit of a professional architectural degree. Weaving together the remaining shreds of my dignity, I returned to Nigeria. It was official: My life was a hopeless failure. As improbable as it seemed, greater problems awaited me at home. My father had been diagnosed with cancer and was given only three months to live. I arrived home to meet him and to help prepare the family for what seemed to be the inevitable. My family, out of desperation, had begun to consult various spiritualists and witch doctors in an attempt to find a cure—all to no avail.

The situation was more than I could bear. Alarmed and confused, I confided in one of my childhood buddies, who encouraged me to talk to his mother. A quiet unassuming English woman, she proved to be a woman of great faith. I poured out my heart to her in a way I'd never spoken with anyone before. I was bitterly disappointed with life—the irony of the fact that the son of a chief justice was a drug addict, my father's hopeless condition and the occult dabbling my family had resorted to in an attempt to save him. With a quiet and calming voice, she shared the gospel with me in a way I'd never heard before, and she told me that I needed to remove the log from my own eye before criticizing my family for the speck in theirs (see Matt. 7:5).

When she had finished, she invited me to pray. As we prayed together she said with more sincerity and authority than I'd ever heard in anyone's voice, "Father." Immediately, the room was filled with the presence of God. She paused for what seemed like an eternity and then said again, "Father." Never before had I experienced the tangible presence of God like I did in that room as wave after wave of His essence washed over me. She prayed for me first in English and then in the strangest language I had ever heard. Rather than alarm me, however, it actually comforted me a great deal.

I left the house that evening and went to a bar with my friend, as was our custom. I knew something was different, but I couldn't quite put my finger on it. We ordered our usual beers and sat down to drink. To my utter amazement, as I attempted to sip my lager, my hand began to shake uncontrollably. On a hunch, I ordered a glass of orange juice. Expecting the same thing to happen, I cautiously brought the glass to my mouth. To my surprise, my hand was as steady as a rock. In disbelief I tried the beer again. This time my hand shook so violently that the drink sloshed out of the glass. My friend watched in amazement as the truth sank in; I was not the same person any more!

The next morning I woke up feeling very ill, almost as if I were reacting to something. As if on cue, in walked a family friend who, unknown to me, had been interceding for me during the past year. (Thank God for praying saints!) He told me this and added that not until the night before had he felt a release to come and talk to me. I told him I needed help and asked him about the strange language my friend's mother had prayed in.

He proceeded to take me through the Scriptures and explained things to me that I'd never heard before. He told me about the baptism in the Holy Spirit. There and then he prayed for me, and I was baptized. Immediately I felt God's power flow through me in an astonishing way. Without delay, I ran to where my father lay and, not really understanding what I was doing, laid my hands on him, praying for his healing. My father recovered and lived another seven years. I was a new man!

The next six months of my life were truly incredible as I felt the sovereign hand of God rest firmly on my life. I had several awesome experiences with the Holy Spirit and walked in some powerful manifestations of the gifts of the Spirit. With this new-found hope and inspiration, I returned to Miami and completed my degree in architecture.

THE CALL TO MINISTRY

Ministry in the church was the furthest thing from my mind when I finally graduated as an architect from the University of

Miami. I loved architecture, and with the prospect of designing buildings for a prestigious Florida firm, life couldn't have been better. Don't get me wrong. I loved God. My pastor at the time, Nick Shubert, of the Miami Sunset Chapel, was a man I greatly admired. However, with a past like mine, I thought God would have to be crazy to call me into ministry! I admit now that at the time I did not fully understand the cleansing power of Calvary!

Much has happened since then, and I've discovered that God has an uncanny knack for taking the most unlikely of people and somehow employing them, despite their apparent inadequacies, to accomplish the most amazing things. As I look back now, these Scriptures found total fulfillment in my personal life:

> He also brought me up out of a horrible pit, out of the miry clay, and set my feet upon a rock, and established my steps (Ps. 40:2).

> And He has made My mouth like a sharp sword; in the shadow of His hand He has hidden Me, and made Me a polished shaft; in His quiver He has hidden me (Isa. 49:2).

> But we have this treasure in earthen vessels, that the excellence of the power may be of God and not of us (2 Cor. 4:7).

Today people often ask what persuaded me to leave a promising career to become a full-time pastor. I simply respond that it was the power of the call. Looking back, I realize that I'd always really known that this is what I was meant to be. I had a deep assurance that the work to which I was called could not fail. This, I believe, is a matter every minister must settle in his or her heart from day one. Did God call you? Set aside the lights, cameras and the expectations of people. Did God call you? When things get rough, as they sometimes do, it's the gentle but firm reassurance of knowing you cannot fail

> *When things get rough, it's the gentle but firm reassurance of knowing you cannot fail because you have been called by God that keeps you from giving up.*

because you have been called by God that keeps you from giving up. The call is never based on credentials, degrees, fame or fortune. God uses broken people, individuals voted least likely to succeed, people just like me.

House on the Rock

If there was one thing I had learned as a young Christian, it was how to pray. I firmly believed the truth of James 5:16: "The effective, fervent prayer of a righteous man avails much." When most of the young men and women in my church were hanging out on the beach, I was praying with the church intercessory prayer team. I knew where I had come from, and there was no way I was going back.

The importance of prayer in all things cannot be overemphasized. When we obeyed God and started House on the Rock, we did not have a whole lot—a motley crew of seven, a widow's living room and no money. This was not your regular fail-safe prescription for beginning a great work of God. What we did have, though, was faith in a sure word from God and the heart to pray. Pray we did! We would often pray from 9:00 P.M. through the night until 7:00 the next morning. We would take a break until 10:00 A.M. and begin praying again until 2:00 P.M. We'd take another break again until 5:00 P.M., and then we prayed until 7:00 P.M. It was not sophisticated, and it was not cute. Our prayers were crude and maybe a bit crazy, but we were totally consumed with the desire to see God's promise to us come to pass.

We didn't know what else to do. If what we were doing didn't work, we had no plan B! However, within a few weeks our group began to grow. Our living room was now too small. We started Sunday morning services in a rented restaurant a few months later. Today, House on the Rock has a membership of over 7,000 people in the mother church, with 36 branch churches spread across Nigeria, Africa and Europe. Prayer continues to be a fundamental part of our ministry. Our prayer pattern has now been modified to follow the hours of the 8 watches of a 24-hour period. We have prayer chains in which each person prays at least 1 hour of every 3-hour prayer watch for a minimum of 4 watches per day. The results of this kind of intense praying speak for themselves, as we have seen incredible growth in all our branches.

A MESSAGE OF HOPE

A man named Chris walked into our service one Sunday morning—he had hit rock bottom. Although we had first met shortly after our church was formed and he had become a member of our intercessory prayer team, unfortunately he left the church, and we lost touch with each other for a few years. The Sunday Chris came back to church, I was shocked to see the state he was in. He had lost virtually everything that he had; and he was, in every sense, a totally broken man. Hearing the message preached that Sunday literally jump-started his life, and he immediately went back to his praying ways. Before long he started a company in the oil and gas sector, which to all intents and purposes was a long shot for success, especially since he had no technical background in the field. God, however, supernaturally brought him into contact with the right people—people who had the right skills and who gave him an extra helping of favor. Today, against all odds, Chris's business is very successful: it has a seven-digit annual cash flow, which in today's Nigerian economy is quite impressive.

Chris is just one example of the many lives that have been changed through the preaching of the gospel of Jesus Christ. We live in rather difficult times; dreams are constantly being dashed against the rocks of adversity. People desperately need to know that things will get better. This is the message of House on the Rock. It is built in large part on the following verse of Scripture: "When my heart is overwhelmed; lead me to the rock that is higher than I" (Ps. 61:2). We preach that there is hope for tomorrow beyond yesterday's failure. There is hope that dead dreams will rise again; there is hope for the weary, the downtrodden, the rejected and the unqualified, because God uses broken people.

We preach that miracles still happen! God still fixes shattered lives. Often, the only thing that prevents a suicide from taking place is one word of hope or comfort. This message of hope transcends race, culture, class and creed. Everybody needs hope. A church that preaches a message that gives people hope, encouragement and healing will never lack for attendance. Does this mean that sin is condoned? Not on your life! When God's Word is preached in its entirety, it is the most balanced guide for daily living known to man.

Characteristically, my personal preaching style is as dynamic and illustrative as possible. I have learned that, as I expound God's Word, if people do not understand me, everyone's time has been wasted. I pay a great deal of attention to clarity and explicitness. God knows what He means, and He means what He says. The more real-life application contained in a message, the more relevant that message becomes to the people.

COMMITMENT TO EXCELLENCE

The face of ministry today has changed somewhat from what it used to be. Today, churches contend with consumer-oriented industries that are driven to meet the demands of a consumer-based society. Our lives are affected by many of these industries, whether we are talking about entertainment, automobiles, computers or fashion. Major industries today are constantly reinventing themselves as they compete for the attention of an image-conscious public. Through interacting with different kinds of people from all kinds of backgrounds, Christian and non-Christian, I have discovered that they have one thing in common: People want to have and be associated with the very best. It does not really matter what it is or whether or not its name can be pronounced. If it has a reputation for being the best, *everybody* wants it!

It is important to understand that God is not just an excellent God; He is the *most* excellent entity in all of existence. Since we are the children of God, whatever we do must reflect the excellence that is God's very nature. Any ministry in our day that is to achieve healthy growth must be committed to excellence. Excellence must be pursued in music, the delivery of the Word, ushering, protocol and, indeed, every other aspect of church life. The world, which is our competition, is committed to a degree of excellence that is sadly missing from many of God's houses. We know that God looks on the heart, but the humans to whom we reach out look on the outward first, long before they get to know what is really in our hearts.

How do we at House on the Rock try to reflect the excellence of God? People walk into our church, and they are often astonished by the degree of care that is put into the many aspects of our services: from the state-of-the-art technical equipment to the décor of the auditorium, the music, the worship, television cameras, lighting and stage sets. Some may question whether all of this is even necessary. We believe that if anything is done for God, it has to be excellent; and if anything carries God's name, it has to be the very best. These are some of the ideals that have inspired us to build a state-of-the-art auditorium and ministry center, assemble what some would say is one of the best choirs in our nation, create the most proficient multimedia presentations available and invest in training and maintaining the most professional staff possible. After all, we are God's representatives. We feel that we must take our responsibility seriously.

A PLAN FOR SUCCESSION

Then Zadok the priest took a horn of oil from the tabernacle and anointed Solomon. Also the king [David] said thus, "Blessed be the LORD God of Israel, who has given one to sit on my throne this day, while my eyes see it!" (1 Kings 1:39,48).

Then it happened, as they continued on and talked, that suddenly a chariot of fire appeared with horses of fire, and separated the two of them; and Elijah went up by a whirlwind into heaven. He also took up the mantle of Elijah that had fallen from him, and went back and stood by the bank of the Jordan (2 Kings 2:11,13).

How is success passed from one generation to the next? In many of the places I have visited, I have observed an apparent gulf between spiritual fathers and their supposed sons.

Whenever there is a powerful move of the Spirit in the older generation, this gulf makes it difficult for the same blessings to continue in the next generation. I was recently speaking with a well-known church leader whom I respect very deeply, and he said something extremely profound: "Paul, you are successful when you can work yourself out of a job." What he meant was that your success is validated when you can hand the work over to someone you have trained and see them do the job better than you.

Our hearts are revealed through our attitude toward succession. Most of us are intimidated by the thought of handing our

Training potential leaders is one way of ensuring that there is continuity between what God did yesterday, what He is doing today and what He will do tomorrow.

ministry over to a successor. We think that once we have turned over our leadership responsibilities, we will no longer be relevant. This could not be further from the truth. The wisdom that we acquire through years of service becomes invaluable in helping a new, young leader avoid the pitfalls. What use is God-given wisdom if the veteran is senile at the time he hands the work over? Lasting progress can only be made through effective succession.

As I have spoken to some church leaders about this, I have realized that we sometimes have a misplaced sense of ownership when it comes to God's work. When I see what God has done through House on the Rock, I need to remind myself that this is His work and not an empire built for the glory of any human being. I am just glad to be part of the adventure.

We have also realized the importance of training potential successors for our leaders at every level. This is just one way of ensuring that there is continuity between what God did yesterday, what He is doing today and what He will do tomorrow. One of the initiatives our ministry has undertaken to encourage healthy relationships between pastors of different ministries and from different generations is the Petra Coalition. The Petra Coalition provides forums for leaders of independent ministries to meet together on a regular basis for seminars, workshops, prayer meetings and fellowship. The aim is to foster strong, relationship-based networks among God's elect.

A RELEVANT CHURCH

The Japanese chef I observed was quite an expert, and the ease with which he wielded his knife with breathtaking speed was truly a wonder to behold. In between the chops and swipes of his blade, he would sprinkle a little salt from the nearby shaker, as he whipped up his house special. I always enjoy a well-prepared meal, and on a good day I have been known to rustle up one or two specialties myself.

Have you ever considered the fact that salt, which is probably the most fundamental of seasonings, is only of value to a chef once it has left the shaker? As long as it stays inside, it does not do anyone or anything any good. In many ways, the Church is similar. I believe the true value of a church only comes into view when it has impacted its community. Beyond attracting large numbers of people on Sundays, every living church needs to be able to affect its environment. Just as the salt that remains in the saltshaker is unprofitable to the cook, a church that cannot affect its neighborhood is of questionable value to the kingdom of God. We are called the "salt of the earth" and the "light of the world" (see Matt. 5:13-14) for a very good reason. Consider the ponderings of the prophet Isaiah as he prophetically defined the heart of God for the nation of Israel and, by implication, for the Church:

> Is this not the fast that I have chosen: to loose the bonds of wickedness, to undo the heavy burdens, to let the oppressed go free, and that you break every yoke? Is it not to share your bread with the hungry, and that you bring to your house the poor who are cast out; when you see the naked, that you cover him, and not hide yourself from your own flesh? (Isa. 58:6-7).

House on the Rock has over the years become involved in a number of community-based projects such as a feeding program for the poor, relief for disaster victims, prison evangelism and rehabilitation of former prisoners. The church has also contributed directly to Nigerian society through the rehabilitation of street gang members known as area boys, the destitute and the needy in the neighborhood. Our new church auditorium is designed to be much more than a church building; it will be a center that caters to several of the growing needs in our community. I believe the days when the church stayed safe behind bolted doors are long gone. In this day and age, the church that is able to transcend race, culture, class and creed to meet a hurting generation at the point of its need is the church that God will use.

TRUE REVIVAL

When John first came to Lagos, he had big dreams but no money. He was so broke that he had to sleep on the floor in one of the shopping malls in the city. That is when we first met. I was just getting ready to plant House on the Rock, and he was launching his company. We hit it off pretty well. He became one of the first members of our church, and a strong friendship began. That was almost 10 years ago. Today, John is the CEO of one of Nigeria's most successful engineering and oil-servicing companies, and he is still on fire for God. Scattered among the congregation of House on the Rock are men and women like John who have been raised up by God in several of the different industries across the country.

These faithful servants are using Christ's principles to galvanize a spiritual revolution in the cities where they live and in the offices where they work. They are the workplace apostles. They have gained apostolic influence in many different sectors of the nation's life and economy, ranging from entertainment to media and from business to the military. They have become a powerful network of people who are committed to spreading this precious gospel to the ends of the nation.

This, I believe, is true revival. Revival is here when the gospel leaps off the pages of the Bible into the hearts of men and women so that they walk out of the confines of a church building into the highways and byways of life in order to reform great nations and bring healing to a hurting generation. We look forward to the days when the Word of God shall be fulfilled on the earth as it is in heaven, to the days when "the kingdoms of this world have become the kingdoms of our Lord and of his Christ, and He shall reign forever and ever!" (Rev. 11:15).

CHAPTER EIGHT

THE MINISTRY AND THE MARKETPLACE

Zach Wazara

Zach Wazara was born in Zimbabwe, where he graduated from the University of Zimbabwe with a bachelor's in business studies. His primary areas of specialization are marketing, corporate finance and management accounting.

Wazara has an extensive background in management, serving as executive director for sales and marketing, chief operating officer and managing director for Econet Wireless Zimbabwe. He also served as chief operating officer for Mascom Wireless in Botswana.

Zach currently serves as CEO of Econet Wireless Nigeria, one of the largest wireless telecommunications companies in the country. He is happily married to Rukudzo and has three daughters and two sons.

Ask Christians in business today why they have built their businesses, and I would guess that over 98 percent would say that they have built them ultimately to bring glory to the name of Christ. They would also tend to add, in the most "spiritual" voice they could muster, that the whole purpose for their generating financial resources is to expand the kingdom of God.

I remember receiving an e-mail from a friend that really challenged me. It accused people of saying that they were running their businesses for the Lord, but when there was a threat of loss, they were quick to protect their names, their egos, their status and other personal interests. The e-mail went on to ask the question, "Is your business truly to glorify Jesus or are you just using the Lord's name as a hiding place to fulfill a personal agenda? If God truly is in it, then why don't you allow God to deal with the threats and let Him be responsible to take the blame when there is any loss suffered?"

This e-mail comes to mind because as I reflect on the experiences we have gone through in our business, I realize just how much the Lord has redefined my understanding of Christian businesspeople and has taught me that it is impossible to speak of being a Christian businessperson without being a workplace apostle. This rule is the same whether you consider your business a Christian business or a business run by Christians, as some like to differentiate.

THE BEGINNING OF THE JOURNEY

I came to Nigeria in April 2001, and my experiences with the Lord and in the workplace in this nation have been awesome! Let me explain by giving my personal testimony of this journey.

As business professionals, my wife and I were very heavily involved with the young adults group called People of Destiny at Hear the Word Ministries in Harare, Zimbabwe. People of Destiny, or PODs, as we were affectionately called, were usually graduates of a fiery youth group and were well grounded in the basics of the Word of God. Our greatest challenge, as with many other young adults, was how to apply the Word to real life situations.

Most of the issues we used to deal with related to the application of the Word in the work environment. This created a sense within me that there was a lot more that business people could do in order to strengthen the Word of God in the business environment. Of course, I did not know then what the Lord had

There was a burning desire within me to see the Church and business linked in a strong and practical way.

in store for me. At one stage I wanted to start an advertising agency called Cornerstone Communication. The agency would tithe and generate money for the Kingdom and do all the other typical things expected of Christian businesses.

Needless to say, there was a burning desire within me to see some activity that linked the Church and business in a strong and practical way. Praying in the workplace seemed to be a good thing, but it did not appear sufficient to me. The senior pastor of Hear the Word Ministries helped me a lot in this regard, because he had a special interest in developing businesspeople. His faith-based teaching, which had a very strong orientation toward reaching out to the nations, had transformed the lives of many businesspeople who attended his church.

In 1997 when I first heard a message about priests and kings in the marketplace, I became extremely excited, because this was the first message I had heard that sought to bring some clarity regarding the relationship between the Christian businessperson and the work of ministry. To my mind, the most important part of the teaching was that the king (understood as the businessperson) had a battlefield on which he had to fight every day in order to conquer. Historically, the battlefield was where war against the Philistines, the Syrians or whatever enemy nation that needed to be confronted was fought. Today's battlefield, however, is the marketplace. What an exciting revelation!

There was a season during which this became the hottest message in most churches in my region of Zimbabwe. However, the emphasis of the message shifted to say that while the priests (local church pastors) would provide the vision (as it was given to them by the Lord), the kings would go out to fight on the battleground and bring back the "spoils of war" to the priests. In other words, the king's role was to provide *provision* for the *vision*.

I must confess that as I traveled around and heard different versions of the workplace message, I felt a bit frustrated by this one interpretation because it seemed to box me in unnecessarily. It clearly was reducing the role that I felt I could play in the marketplace to just providing resources for the local church. I noted that it created a serious conflict, not only in me, but also in fellow Christian businesspeople. It was as though the only other way you could contribute to the kingdom of God besides contributing money was to become a pastor, either full-time or part-time.

ECONET WIRELESS INTERNATIONAL

On a positive note, I had received a good bit of spiritual satisfaction from what was happening in the company that I work for, Econet Wireless International. Econet is a mobile telephone company that was established in 1994 in Harare, Zimbabwe. Strive Masiyiwa, an outstanding entrepreneur whose core business at that time was construction, decided to move into telecommunications.

It turned out that the new company would face one of the fiercest court battles in Africa in order to deregulate Zimbabwe's telecommunications industry. The government in Zimbabwe was of the opinion that private sector players could not be trusted with operating in such a sensitive and strategic sector. Strive, to the contrary, felt that he had every right as a businessman to establish a business of his choice, particularly given the fact that there was a need to expand telecommunications in the country in order to support the burgeoning industry and population. The only way to break the impasse was to declare that the government's position was in breach of the constitutional right of freedom of speech. One must understand that challenging the government at that time was something that no private citizen had ever attempted, especially in view of the fact that the same government had spearheaded the country's political independence from the British 14 years earlier. Consequently, the government regarded this as a slap in the face and a sign of disloyalty and rebellion. To make things worse, it was coming from a black man in a nation fraught with racial tensions.

The government responded with all the political and institutional resources they could muster in an attempt to stop Strive and Econet. This marked the beginning of a long battle, which lasted four years. By 1996, the company had a fully operational mobile system in Harare, the nation's capital, as well as a core staff of about 54 people, which included some expatriates. The authorities, however, would not permit Econet to sign up any customers.

Strive Masiyiwa, who is a born-again, Spirit-filled believer, led the company through one of the toughest periods of his professional life. His entire construction empire collapsed until there was nothing left. Undaunted, he declared that the Lord had given him a vision in which Econet would provide telecommunications to all the peoples of Africa.

A Season of Wilderness

With every passing month, things appeared to get worse. The government introduced new laws, explicitly designed to obstruct the growth of Econet. Banks were discouraged covertly, as well as overtly, from financing the company, which was perceived as funding an enemy of the state. The government-owned telephone company was granted permission to start operating a mobile telephone division in late 1996 as a way of emphasizing that there would be no need for privately operated mobile communication services.

During early 1997, bids were solicited as the politicians considered the admission of private operators into the government-run mobile communications sector. Naturally, the contract was awarded to a consortium of black-empowerment political activists who supported the government, in spite of a clearly superior bid submitted by Econet. In fact, Econet allegedly came last among the five or six bidders that participated. This open rejection of Econet was followed by threats to shut down the mobile system and to confiscate the equipment. The pressure was unwavering.

It became clear to us at Econet that as we endured these trials we were making our wilderness walk from Egypt to the Promised Land. We embarked on a season of continuous prayer and fasting, anchored around a daily morning devotional for all staff that could attend, led by Strive Masiyiwa himself. Chain-fasting, where a group of staff would fast for 24 hours and then another group would fast for the next 24 hours, complemented this daily devotional. This process at times would go on for months. Members of a number of local churches who worked outside the company often joined in praying for us, as they all desired to see justice prevail and the blatant corruption surrounding the case defeated and uprooted.

A significant number would also participate in the all-night prayer meetings held at Strive's house every Friday night. This weekly prayer meeting was held for four years. As churches learned about the case from newspapers and friends, more and more intercessors from around the country joined our cause. Since we were operating a mobile network with no customers (which meant no revenue), the Word of God became our only source of sustenance. The Lord provided incredible opportunities for our faith to be stretched, enabling the company to stand strong in the face of all kinds of adversity. Many supernatural miracles affected all of us at Econet at both corporate and individual levels. As a result, the company continued to have a highly motivated staff in spite of the fact that salaries were paid only sporadically. One of the greatest opportunities for our faith to grow concerned the Botswana mobile license.

THE BOTSWANA LICENSE

As I mentioned, during this difficult season, the Lord sent men and women who would pray with us and encourage us. Among them was a young man named Prince Mandizha, who at the time worked for the Harare City Council. Prince was an intercessor, and he carried an enormous burden for Econet. The Lord was using him in quite an extraordinary way and would show him visions of things that would happen sooner or later concerning "the battle," as we had come to refer to our trial.

In June of 1997, at the peak of our struggle for the Zimbabwe license, Prince came to see Strive with a word from the Lord. The Lord was saying that Econet should put in a bid for the mobile phone license being floated for auction in the neighboring nation of Botswana. Every indicator in the industry said that this was a foolish thing to do, especially in view of the intense political, regulatory and financial constraints the company had been facing. After another round of corporate prayer and fasting, Strive left for Botswana to scout out the prospects and to get a better feel for what we should do.

The Botswana regulator advised him that the tender had been published in May of that year and that prequalification meetings had already been held with interested operators, including giants like France Telecom, Bharti Cellular of India and Vodacom and MTN of South Africa, the latter two being the first and second largest mobile operators in Africa. Strive's response when he came back was, "The Lord has given this into our hands." And that was the beginning of a living testimony.

The Botswana regulator required that any bidder should have considerable operating experience and a customer base of at least 500,000 subscribers. Heavy financial guarantees running into several million American dollars were also required to support any technical submission. We, of course, did not satisfy any of these conditions—at least not in the natural—but by faith we continued to process our bid documents under conditions I can only describe as miraculous.

ANSWERED PRAYER

We encouraged ourselves with a variety of Scriptures and continued to declare, according to the prophecy, that the contract would be ours. The Lord provided us with a technical partner less than a week before the deadline for the bids. We completed preparation of the documents with only two days to spare. Each of the 12 required copies had Isaiah 40:31 on the front cover:

> But those who wait on the Lord, shall renew their strength; they shall mount up with wings like eagles, they shall run and not be weary, they shall walk and not faint.

We prayed Nehemiah 6:15-16 over the documents and sent them to Botswana.

> So the wall was finished on the twenty-fifth day of Elul, in fifty-two days. And it happened, when all our enemies heard of it, and all the nations around us saw these things, that they were very disheartened in their own eyes; for they perceived that this work was done by our God.

This was an incredible statement of faith, since we still did not have any of the required financial guarantees. It is hard to believe, but only two hours before the bids were to be opened, we were able to stuff into our 12 packets the pages documenting our financial guarantees.

Against all odds, in 1998 we came in first against the bids of the world and continental giants. I was the chief operating officer of the company during its first year of operation, and our experiences with the Lord at that time could be the subject of another book. We launched the network in less than 35 days, since we had been asked by the Botswana regulator to make the network ready for President Bill Clinton, who was visiting the country for the first time. Our very first customers were President Bill Clinton's entourage and the American Embassy in Botswana!

Today, Mascom Wireless (our founding company) remains the biggest mobile network in Botswana with an excess of 70 percent market share and an amazing 300,000 customers in a country with a population of roughly 1.3 million.

EXTENDED BORDERS

Back in Zimbabwe, it was not until late 1997 that the high court declared Econet duly licensed to operate its mobile network in the country. We had fought the legal battle, and finally we had come out of the wilderness. The network was launched in 1998, two years after the government network had been started. Furthermore, a second competitor had entered the business.

We continued with prayer and fasting, this time regarding the battle to occupy what we saw to be the Promised Land. We prayed about every single aspect of the network, customers, capacity, favor with suppliers, finances, etc. We received amazing blessings from the Lord. Customers loved our cause and within six months we had become the largest telecommunications operator in the country.

In January 2000, Strive Masiyiwa came into one of our Econet morning prayer meetings and said that the Lord had strongly impressed a Scripture in his spirit:

Ask of Me, and I will give You the nations for Your inheritance, and the ends of the earth for Your possession (Ps. 2:8).

I remarked that this was a confirmation of what the Lord had spoken to me a year before. At that time, however, I had not received a revelation of its significance. We immediately convened a corporate chain fast, which, unknown to us at the time, was to last almost nine months. Strive soon concluded that this was the Lord's appointed time for us to start Econet's international operations. In March 2000, by faith, he sent one of our colleagues—a faithful, God-fearing man named Marco Signorin—to set up our Econet Wireless International headquarters in Johannesburg, South Africa.

By the end of 2000, the Lord had indeed shown His faithfulness, taking the company beyond the borders of Zimbabwe. Econet had established mobile, Internet, satellite and fixed network interests in various countries including the United Kingdom, Morocco, New Zealand, Lesotho and South Africa, in addition to the already established networks in Zimbabwe and Botswana.

OUR VISION TO CHANGE THE WORLD

Long before this time, we had recognized through our direct experiences and through the many prophetic messages that we continued to receive both corporately and individually that the Lord had set us on a spiritual course in which He was using Econet as a vehicle. We also had long realized that the character and ethics of the business had to be aligned with the Word of God, just as He had proclaimed through various prophetic utterances. From our experiences, it was clear that He was calling us and had "this day set [us] over the nations and over the kingdoms, to root out and to pull down, to destroy and to throw down, to build and to plant" (Jer. 1:10).

In late 2000, we changed our corporate slogan from "Econet Wireless—Your Cellular Network" to one that better articulates the role that we believe God has given us, namely, to change and transform our continent of Africa. The new corporate slogan became "Inspired to Change Your World." This is what we really stand for. First, we are inspired by God Himself. Second, in order to bring about change, there has to be a transformation through the power of the Holy Spirit. Finally "our world" is a direct reference to every aspect of the people we serve, including spirit, soul and body.

Our experiences with the Lord in all the markets He had opened for us and the incredible miracles and testimonies that accompanied them formed the basis upon which we responded to a prophetic call to enter into the giant of the African market, Nigeria. This leads to the reason that my story belongs in a book on the extension of God's kingdom in Nigeria.

A HISTORICAL PERSPECTIVE OF AFRICA'S GIANT

Nigeria is an extremely interesting nation for many reasons:

- It is the most populous state in Africa, with over 130 million people. In fact, it is said that one in every five black people worldwide is Nigerian.
- It is the sixth largest producer of oil in the world and is endowed with many other natural resources, including a massive potential for agriculture.
- Its marketplace is so large and accommodating that one would have to make a concerted effort for the average business enterprise to fail.
- It has a cash economy; therefore, where the business systems are properly structured, there is no such thing as bad debt.
- Because of oil revenue, its foreign exchange reserves are quite strong compared to those of other African countries; therefore, the exchange rate remains fairly stable.

Yet this same country had been plagued by years of military rule before the restoration of democracy in May 1999. The net effect of military rule was the stagnation—if not outright regression—of the development of one of the most beautiful countries in Africa. Foreign investors were kept at bay, as political instability made it difficult for any foreign investor to commit long-term cash investments. The middle class was inexorably squeezed out of the economy and, in numerous cases, out of the country, as the productive sector stopped growing. This state of affairs birthed a culture in which everyone held a short-term view about the future. The banking sector would only support projects for businesses that would repay most of their loan within 180 days.

This, in turn, created an environment in which people began placing their earnings into savings accounts—abroad! The absence of accountability at federal, state and local levels devastated the country's infrastructure, removing the abilities both to expand and to maintain the economy. Contracts would be awarded and then canceled after the project had begun, with no legal recourse. The related corruption and breakdown in law and order also bred a crop of well-educated, unemployed and extremely frustrated citizens. Even worse were the chilling accounts of pain and loss suffered at the hands of corrupt customs officials at Nigerian airports, accounts that visitors from southern Africa would report to us.

MY JOURNEY TO NIGERIA

To go or not to go? That was the question, and it wasn't an easy one to answer. I vividly recall my own personal fears, and all of us at Econet tried to sidestep any possibility of being assigned to Nigeria. As an example, as CEO of Econet Wireless Zimbabwe, I had suggested that my chief technical officer, Bernard

Fernandes, be part of the project team in Nigeria. He reacted rather violently to the suggestion and accused me of trying to get rid of him. He stated that he would rather resign than face a stint in Nigeria. Today, however, things have changed. Bernard is still faithfully serving as chief technical officer for Econet Wireless—in Nigeria! He knows every nook and cranny of the country like the back of his hand, and he even may be beginning to love it.

In October 2000, it was my turn to visit Nigeria on a scouting mission. It was my first trip—and it was only for a few days. After that visit, I apologized profusely to Bernard for my insensitivity to his future in nominating him to move to Nigeria. It was my turn to mumble something to Strive Masiyiwa about the importance of my remaining in Zimbabwe for the well-being of the company. I also suggested that he explain to me what I had done wrong to deserve being "exiled" to Nigeria for this short trip. It goes without saying that I have since come to regret those negative attitudes, and I have repented to God on numerous occasions for my lack of faith and vision.

I began to prepare the initial business plan, which was required for the Nigerian digital mobile license auction, planned for late 2000 or early 2001. In my mind, I was doing this as part of my role as one of the directors of the group.

The Lord had told me in September and again in October 2000 that He would be taking me to a foreign country, and He had given me a very broad overview of what would happen. I concluded that He must have been referring to my relocation to our corporate headquarters in South Africa. I had written down both messages in my journal and had promptly forgotten about them. On New Year's Eve 2000, I was at Hear the Word Ministries' all-night celebration, and as the group began praying and thanking the Lord for bringing us into the new millennium, a man came to me and began to speak prophetically concerning what the Lord was showing him regarding me. He stated that the Lord would be taking me to a foreign country and proceeded to outline everything that the Lord had shown me concerning His plans for me in 2001. I thanked him and said quietly, "South Africa, here I come."

In April 2001, I was to visit Nigeria for two weeks. My assignment was to travel back and forth to help launch Econet Wireless Nigeria. Then I would move with my family to our corporate headquarters in South Africa. Ironically, I am still on the longest two-week journey of my life.

On the second night of my visit to Nigeria, God gave me a vision in which I saw a huge billboard inscribed with the words of Jeremiah 1:10:

> See, I have this day set you over the nations and over the kingdoms, to root out and to pull down, to destroy and to throw down, to build and to plant.

It was awesome. I wanted to obey God, but I still needed full revelation of the significance of the vision. I was soon to discover that I had just entered a spiritual boot camp.

THE CHURCH IN NIGERIA

The more time I spent in Nigeria, the more I began to realize that in the midst of all the bad press Nigeria seems to get, there existed a well-organized and rapidly expanding spiritual revolution that was set to sweep away all of the corruption and misadministration of the past. This revival has been unparalleled in any other nation on the earth.

One interesting phenomenon I observed in Nigeria was the number of businesses with Christian names or with Scriptures over their entrances. Even more astounding was the sheer number and sizes of the churches in the country. In some places, I noticed as many as 10 churches on a single street. I was taken to Winners Chapel to see the marvel of a 50,400-seat auditorium—the world's largest—which is filled with on-fire believers every Sunday.

Attending the all-night prayer meeting of the Redeemed Christian Church of God (RCCG) that meets on the first Friday of every month required a paradigm shift for someone

> *God spoke to us that Econet Wireless was part of God's plan to transform the continent of Africa, to establish His kingdom on Earth and to bring glory to Himself. Wow!*

like me who had never seen a half million people gathered together at one time to pray. And they do this every month! As though this were not enough, the end-of-year Holy Ghost Congress, also hosted by the RCCG, attracts an estimated 6 to 7 million people during a one-week period! How awesome is that?

I would constantly ask myself whether the vast numbers were also representative of the quality of their spiritual experiences and whether people's lives were changed by the impact of the church. The questions continued to plague me, but they were not things I could comfortably ask anyone without being thoroughly misunderstood. I continued to mull this over in my mind, as there appeared to be something missing. Then came the beginning of my own spiritual experience, which would begin to shed light on the missing piece of the puzzle.

The first time I met the general overseer of the RCCG, Pastor Enoch A. Adeboye (undoubtedly the most humble man I know), he stated that he did not have much to say to me except that at 2:00 P.M. on December 25, 1979, the Lord had spoken to him about men whom He would raise up for the transformation of the continent of Africa, to establish His kingdom on Earth and to bring glory to Himself. He stated to me that the Econet vision was a part of this plan. Wow!

A NIGERIAN BUSINESS PARADIGM

Doing business in Nigeria has to be one of the most challenging experiences ever. One must understand that the business culture in Nigeria is completely different from that of any other country on Earth.

From a telecommunications perspective, we were coming into a country whose teledensity was third to the lowest in the world, with only Mongolia's and Afghanistan's being lower. There were only 420,000 fixed lines to service 130 million people. Nigeria's basic infrastructure to support the launch of our network—such as power, transmission and road access to certain parts of the country—was nonexistent, requiring some very innovative ideas. At the same time, the demand for telephone service was so high that no network could cope with the requests for service. Plus a lot of training was required to prepare local staff to handle cellular telephone technology. Econet and its major market competitor have had to put in huge amounts of work in order to introduce an additional 2 million telephone subscribers over just two years of operation.

We have seen our telephone company physically transform the economy of Nigeria, as we have done the following:

- Created employment, both directly and indirectly
- Trained local staff in the high-tech skills required to implement a successful cellular telephone business
- Revitalized the banking industry through high-volume, high-value transactions, as we have brought in foreign direct investment and equipment in excess of $1.5 billion over a two-year period
- Rapidly expanded the construction industry, as they are responsible for building our masts
- Introduced new social services, such as the Econet Crisis Center, which will in the future become a pillar in the health care delivery system
- Revitalized the large informal sector, which contributes over 50 percent of all Nigerian economic activity, bringing in greater efficiency through telephony in a sector that was largely dependent on road transportation for communication and movement of goods
- Linked Nigeria much more effectively to the rest of the world—prior to 2001, only 18 percent of telephone calls made to Nigeria were successfully patched through; today, call completion has increased to over 65 percent

It has been extremely gratifying to see measurable progress toward the transformation of a nation because of the work that we have done in the telecommunications sector by the Lord's leading.

INSIDE OF ECONET WIRELESS NIGERIA

Prior to my arrival in Nigeria, my greatest fear was working in a company that would emulate the character of the many corrupt institutions and corporations I had heard and read about. I was convinced that from the outset we needed to put in place foundations of righteousness if we were to fulfill our divine vision and mission statement derived from Psalm 2:8.

This was no easy task, as it required hiring the right people—an extremely difficult undertaking in a foreign nation with a completely different cultural mind-set and an extremely fast-paced and unforgiving business environment. Part of the process included institutionalizing anticorruption policies to minimize the incidences of bribery and corruption. More important, I had to set up intercessory prayer teams both within the company as well as through the local churches. We have established these same practices in every other country where we operate.

We pray about practically everything. We have prayed for additional capacity on our equipment, and God has expanded our switching capacity. We have prayed for God to intervene when the network developed major faults and the engineers could not figure out what the problem was, and God fixed the problem. We have prayed for favor with the banks, and we raised $80 million over a three-week period, with $140 million in other loans being simultaneously restructured from 180-day facilities to 4-year facilities with a 12-month moratorium. We have prayed for additional customers and have sold the equivalent of 140,000 lines in three days. Without a doubt, we have seen the power of God move in our company! We have prayed for favor with the press, especially during some of the most protracted shareholder disputes any company could go through. We have survived these battles, and the press has been inexplicably favorable toward us.

Prayer and the seemingly instantaneous answers to prayer have strengthened the faith of the staff that believe in and confess Jesus as Lord. It has astounded those who do not share our faith in Jesus.

In the midst of all these apparent miracles, the question still lingered in my mind, Lord, what is the link between my work and Your work, about which You have spoken to me so frequently?

Marketplace Apostles

When apostle C. Peter Wagner came to Nigeria, I received a revelation concerning the marketplace ministry. I understood that the Church in Nigeria had been extremely effective in bringing people to the knowledge of Christ, which explained its massive growth in numbers. Yet I sensed something was lacking. And then the revelation came: The missing link was the marketplace, or workplace, apostle.

The workplace apostle continues the work of the nuclear church when it signs off on Sunday (metaphorically speaking). Working in consonance with the fivefold ministry, the marketplace apostle accomplishes the following:

- Interfaces with the nuclear church in order to maintain relevance in the community
- Creates opportunities for the gospel to impact secular society
- Sets up systems and structures for societal transformation (banks, schools, etc.)
- Develops workplace leaders and role models
- Mentors others in order to create a lasting legacy
- Builds enduring institutions that create positive societal change
- Transfers large amounts of wealth to the nuclear church to enable it to fulfill its role in the community

Throughout the New Testament, we find record of men and women in the marketplace who impacted the lives of the people as they extended their spheres of influence beyond the borders of the synagogues and the temples. In Acts 17–19, we read how Paul taught in the synagogues and in the marketplace and experienced the joy of leading numerous successful and influential people to the knowledge of Jesus.

It is in this realization that freedom to walk fully in our calling and purpose comes. It is in the knowledge that there is no real dividing line between ministry and the marketplace that we, as nonpulpit ministers in the marketplace, are able not only to win converts but also to raise disciples.

As the plans and purposes of God continue to unfold in my life, the story is still being written. I am recognizing more and more the purpose for my being in the Nigerian marketplace. How incredible that I be given the opportunity through the establishing of Econet Wireless Nigeria to somehow participate in the grand plan of transforming Africa's most populous and indeed most powerful state for the glory of God.

CHAPTER NINE

BRINGING LIGHT TO THE MUSLIMS

Emmanuel Nuhu Kure

A man divinely endowed with a peculiar anointing to prepare the Church and the nations at large for the return of the King of glory, Emmanuel Nuhu Kure is the vision coordinator of the Throneroom (TRUST) Ministry in Kafanchan, Kaduna State, Nigeria. A prophetic voice to the nations, Kure has established ministry branches in all the major cities of Nigeria as well as in many other countries.

Kure has served as the national coordinator of associate traveling secretaries and senior friends of Nigeria Fellowship of Evangelical Students as well as former Calvary Ministry chapter coordinator for Kafanchan.

He is a member of the advisory board of Pentecostal Fellowship of Nigeria and also a national adviser for Aglow International, Nigeria. Kure has a degree in mass communications and is well traveled internationally.

Emmanuel, his wife and their children live in Kafanchan.

Ever since the nineteenth century, there has been an ongoing battle for the soul of northern Nigeria. I was born at a time when my parents were fighting for a sense of belonging and an identity that would provide a secure future. The reason for their struggle was the fact that they come from a minority tribe in Kaduna State in north central Nigeria, where most people were either Catholic or an animistic spirit worshiper. However, the state government was largely Muslim controlled, as were many other governments in the North. For that reason, my parents were not allowed to pursue post-high school studies or attend teacher training college unless they were willing to convert to Islam.

THE BLOOD OF MARTYRS

Much innocent blood has been shed as a result of religious conflicts in northern Nigeria. However, things are changing. A spiritual awakening is arising from the embers of persecution and death. The story of northern Nigeria is not unlike that of the Early Church, where, according to Acts 8 and 9, the Church paid the price for its existence with the blood of innocent martyrs like Stephen. While it is true that Nigeria is experiencing unprecedented manifestations of revival in terms of enormous gatherings and spiritual awakening, the revival in the North is still at the foundational stage. The Church in the North is becoming knit together by the Holy Spirit in a revival of unity and prayer borne from its common suffering. That is the story I want to tell in this chapter.

For the flimsiest of reasons, militant Islamic fundamentalists often viciously attack the Church. Christians are killed at random in an attempt to completely wipe out the Church in the predominantly Muslim North and to declare that the North is completely Muslim territory, an extension of the Arab Middle Eastern world. Typical northern Nigerian Muslims are more connected to their Arab Islamic identity than to their Nigerian heritage. For them, the Islamic laws of Sharia are more sacred than the laws of the land. This is why the idea of the Church being alive and well in the northern states of Nigeria is anathema to Muslims. From infancy, Muslim children are taught to hate the Christian Church and to fear the danger that Christianity represents in secularizing the fundamental values of the Koran. They are taught to despise all Jews and not to trust the *kafiri* (infidels, or non-Muslims) but instead to kill them as a duty to Allah. From the time children begin to speak their first words, the training begins.

The situation has gone from bad to worse. Every thought or idea expressed publicly, and sometimes even in private, that can be seen as contrary to Islamic tradition is met with brutal force, sometimes death. Non-Muslims live very suppressed lives. Worse still is the threat that evangelism of any kind among Muslims will be punished with death; it is even banned in some northern states. Muslim converts to Christianity face being ostracized from their families, and many go into hiding, only to be hunted by their families for the rest of their lives, facing certain death if found.

One such convert to Christianity, Yunusa, died in my uncle Marshal's family house in Zonkwa, poisoned by a close childhood friend of his who had found out where he was living. In the few years he had been alive as a Christian, he had witnessed fearlessly about his newfound faith and had won many to Christ. He succeeded in moving from place to place, hiding from his family until he was finally found and killed. This story is representative of everyday life in northern Nigeria and of the tensions with which we believers must live.

In 1987, as a result of the open preaching about Jesus at a college of education in Kafanchan, the third largest town in Kaduna State, about 150 churches were burned down by Muslims; and the lives of thousands, most of whom were Christians, were lost in greater Kaduna alone. Christian seminaries like the Baptist seminary in Kawo, Kaduna, were destroyed; pastors were burned alive; and in some cases, whole families were wiped out. The loss of property alone was estimated to be in the millions of dollars. It was the worst religious crisis on record in the entire history of Nigeria. The grief was far-reaching. One would have been hard pressed to find even one Christian family not personally affected by the tragic loss of lives. I was well acquainted with some of those who died as martyrs, professing Jesus to the end.

This tragedy forever changed the spiritual landscape of Nigeria. It revealed the huge religious chasm that previously existed, creating the enormous spiritual tension in present-day Nigeria. This single event finally served to open the eyes of the South to the plight and realities of the overwhelming persecution faced by the Church in the North. It also provoked a deep move of the Holy Spirit in the North.

THE JOY OF SUFFERING

As the persecution and tensions escalated, sometimes whole villages had to be moved from one place to another because they were non-Muslim settlements judged to be too close to Muslim villages. This kind of forced migration was commonplace in the Gombe area. If they resisted the pressures to relocate their villages, non-Muslims became targets of constant attacks that included the destruction of their farmland, their cattle and indeed their lives.

I grew up in an era when discrimination in the educational and civil service sectors against Christians and animists in the North was high. I was refused entry to study my preferred course at the university I had applied to, because I had a Christian name. This overt prejudice prevailed despite my official letter from the joint admission and matriculation board accepting me to study mass communications at Bayero University. Conversely, all the Hausa Muslims, even those less qualified than I, were granted admission to study whatever they chose. Even Christians who somehow were admitted and graduated encountered a glass ceiling in the job market, above which they could never rise.

Regardless of the apparent hardships and the prejudice displayed against me, I was determined to follow God's calling to preach the gospel, irrespective of the consequences. I determined that nobody would keep me down as long as there was breath left in my body. Along with friends of mine who were also committed Christians, we set out to fight the system through spiritual warfare, prayer and evangelism. We made the decision that, for us, to live was to reflect Christ entirely—even if it meant death—because, according to Philippians 1:21, to die was our gain.

I have endured no fewer than nine physical attempts on my life. Sadly, I have buried a number of my minister friends who were victims of religious fanaticism. One of them, for example, was asked by Muslims to renounce his faith. When he refused, his house—with him still inside—was set on fire. He died singing loudly to his God.

There is a happier story of Idi Kano, a Muslim convert whom I was privileged to know personally. He continued to live among his people after his conversion, refusing to run away in spite of all the persecution and attempts on his life. God supernaturally

God is well able to subdue the spiritual principalities of northern Nigeria, preserving His Church even during wicked persecution.

kept him alive with great signs and wonders, making him a role model and pillar of strength for all the saints in the North. He finally died of natural causes at a ripe old age. Idi Kano was a major inspiration in my life, and his testimony affirmed the fact that God was well able to subdue the principalities of the North, preserving His Church even during wicked persecution.

Before his death, this great man of God would station himself in the heart of the city of Kano. Standing in Kano's open markets, he would proclaim Jesus with all his might and call all Muslims to repent or risk facing eternal damnation. He refused to move out of his house, and try as they might, Muslim fanatics were not able to kill him. Idi Kano and a few others like him made us believe that it was possible to serve God victoriously without fear in the North.

A KINDLED FLAME

Divine revelation through numerous prophetic words caused my spirit to burn with the recognition that God was set to do a mighty work in the North if we would have childlike faith in Him. The testimonies of fearless men like Idi Kano fired me up to believe that even in the desert North, God would make all things possible. There were several of us who together determined to lay our lives on the line and to step out in faith. Our stated mission was to reopen northern Nigeria to God's divine power and love. We were ready to confront the behemoth of Islam in Nigeria.

We began traveling from city to city, visiting numerous strategic Islamic sites. At these sacred sites, we would prophesy over the land, demanding that it keep God's Sabbath of peace for the righteous according to Ezekiel 34:25-26:

> I will make a covenant of peace with them, and cause wild beasts to cease from the land; and they will dwell safely in the wilderness and sleep in the woods. I will make them and the places all around My hill a blessing; and I will cause showers to come down in their season; there shall be showers of blessing.

We began to hold open prayer campaigns and prayer and prophecy conferences to address issues such as the role of the Church in northern Nigeria, salvation and the second coming of the Lord Jesus Christ. We held large prayer events to seek God for territorial deliverance. Tribal people did identificational repentance, and we rededicated the land to God. Through this, untold numbers have come to the saving knowledge of Jesus Christ. We determined not to hold our peace until the land began to open and the spiritual atmosphere began to change. We continue these things today.

The land is opening up! Biblical evangelical churches are experiencing great revivals. Believers are becoming open to the promptings and desires of the Holy Spirit. Muslims are beginning to repent all over the North as unexpected dramatic visitations of the Holy Spirit occur on a daily basis. Of course, there are times when the immense stresses and strains of Muslim pressure still seek to overwhelm and discourage us. However, we constantly recognize that God is our very present help in times of need and He has never left or forsaken us.

OUR PROPHETIC FOUNDATION

Prophetic prayer action and the resilience of the Church became the foundation on which the spiritual gate of the Church began to open. This spiritual revolution was predicated on the following verses of Scripture:

> Prophesy to the mountains of Israel [the deserts of Northern Nigeria], and say, "O mountains of Israel, hear the word of the LORD! Thus says the Lord GOD: 'Because the enemy has said of you, "Aha! The ancient heights have become our possession,"'" therefore prophesy, and say, "Thus says the Lord GOD: 'Because they made you desolate and swallowed you up on every side, so that you became the possession of the rest of the nations, and you are taken up by the lips of talkers and slandered by the people'—therefore, O mountains of Israel, hear the word of the Lord GOD! Thus says the Lord GOD to the mountains, the hills, the rivers, the valleys, the desolate wastes, and the cities that have been forsaken, which became plunder and mockery to the rest of the nations all around—therefore thus says the Lord GOD: 'Surely I have spoken in My burning jealousy against the rest of the nations and against all Edom, who gave My land to themselves as a possession, with wholehearted joy and spiteful minds, in order to plunder its open country.' . . .

'But you, O mountains of Israel [northern Nigeria], you shall shoot forth your branches and yield your fruit to My people Israel [the Church], for they are about to come. For indeed I am for you, and I will turn to you, and you shall be tilled and sown. I will multiply men upon you, all the house of Israel [the Church], all of it; and the cities shall be inhabited and the ruins rebuilt . . . Yes, I will cause men to walk on you, My people Israel [the Church]; they shall take possession of you, and you shall be their inheritance; no more shall you bereave them of children.' Thus says the Lord GOD: 'Because they say to you, "You devour men and bereave your nation of children," therefore you shall devour men no more, nor bereave your nation [tribes] anymore,' says the Lord GOD. 'Nor will I let you hear the taunts of the nations anymore, . . . nor shall you cause your nation to stumble anymore,' says the Lord GOD" (Ezek. 36:1-15).

In obedience to the Lord, we began literally to proclaim these words to the North.

THE BELIEVERS IN THE GAP

Part of our strategy in prophesying to the land is to encourage elders who are 50 years of age and older to stand before the Lord continually, publicly representing the ancient covenants and those who made them.

At the age of fifty years they must cease performing this work, and shall work no more. They may minister with their brethren in the tabernacle of meeting, to attend to needs, but they themselves shall do no work. Thus you shall do to the Levites regarding their duties (Num. 8:25-26).

These elders stand as a bridge for the younger generation so that the effects of the Word of God on the land will continue to the next generation. They also stand symbolically because the Scriptures teach that elders govern with God in heaven, to confess the sins of the forefathers and the sons and to reconcile God with the land.

> Around the throne were twenty-four thrones, and on the thrones I saw twenty-four elders sitting, clothed in white robes; and they had crowns of gold on their heads (Rev. 4:4).

They also profess God as King over their lands, as was the practice in the days of Joshua, when they proclaimed that they would have no other gods ruling over them.

We also encourage the women to become involved in prayer, breaking every snare of the witchcraft of "women who sew magic charms on their sleeves" (Ezek. 13:18) and of their harlotry. They stand in the gap as the wailing women spoken of in Jeremiah 9:17-19:

> Thus says the LORD of hosts: "Consider and call for the mourning women, that they may come; and send for skillful wailing women, that they may come. Let them make haste and take up a wailing for us, that our eyes may run with tears, and our eyelids gush with water. For a voice of wailing is heard from Zion: 'How we are plundered! We are greatly ashamed, because we have forsaken the land, because we have been cast out of our dwellings.'"

Finally, we get the congregation—all the people—to confess together personal sins relating to the land. The Lord has never failed to reopen whole cities after these prophetic actions have been carried out on site. We then release pastors and evangelists to take over the cities and continue the work of discipleship where we have left off.

WARFARE IN THE SPIRIT REALM

Friday, the Muslim day of prayer, is a spiritual gate by which Christians can enter into warfare against the spirit of Islam. Every Friday we rise before 5:00 A.M. to lift up a cry of judgment against every throne, or principality, that may be

The Church worldwide must begin a concerted and coordinated prayer siege against Islam on its holy day so that the gospel of the Kingdom is not hindered in the nations.

released through the traditional Friday prayers of Islam. The Lord revealed to us that it is on Fridays that dominion for the entire week is established. He showed us that the kingdom of darkness seeks to establish control in the spirit realm through the efficacy of Islamic Friday prayers. We were made to understand that through these prayers, Muslims sow the seeds of the dominion of Allah over cities and nations. Indeed, they seek to control or dictate situations in the spirit realm over those cities and nations. This is why it is typically after the jumat mosque prayers that most of the agitation and violence takes place in many parts of the world, especially in the Islamic nations.

The Lord showed us that if we would battle in prayer against those principalities and powers on Fridays, then we would be able to establish control in the spirit realm against their diabolical workings. We believe that this word from the Lord is not just for Nigeria. The Church worldwide must begin a concerted and coordinated prayer siege against Islam on its holy day so that the gospel of the Kingdom is not hindered in the nations. The Church must also pray for the salvation of Muslims on that day; such prayer has proved effective. Through prayer and spiritual warfare, we can reverse all the occult manipulations by the spirit of Islam and pray the truths of the kingdom of God over the lives of Islam's followers.

PROPHETIC EVANGELISM

Among unreached people groups, to whom the gospel has never been preached, we carry out prophetic evangelism. Much fruit is seen after such prophetic prayer sessions. As the people are converted to Christ, we plant churches in those regions and disciple leaders who will be given the responsibility to take the gospel to the rest of their people groups. We have done this quite effectively in parts of northern Cameroon where the Lord is helping to check the spread of Islam. God told us that if we would sow into the northern area of Cameroon, a densely populated Muslim region, He would in turn raise up a harvest of souls in northern Nigeria. In other areas within Nigeria where we have seen fruit from prophetic evangelism, we hand over the coordinating of discipleship efforts to missions organizations or churches that partner with us in ministry.

MIRACULOUS MUSLIM CONVERTS

The results of our prophetic prayer and evangelism are spectacular testimonies of conversion. You see, among the Fulani

Muslims, once the head of a clan gives his life to Christ, there is a high likelihood that the rest of the clan will follow suit. We have seen whole villages turn to Christ. The most spectacular aspect of it all is the fact that in many cases nobody preaches to them. Because the spiritual veil of darkness over the people group has been broken by strategic prayer, Jesus often reveals Himself sovereignly to the people through divine revelations and physical manifestations of power. At times He even uses their own holy book, the Koran, to talk to them and then instructs them to meet with a specific Christian brother for guidance on what to do next.

Some powerful Muslim converts have been birthed into the kingdom of God through such miraculous experiences. Today, many of them are anointed ministers of the gospel in Nigeria. We are in touch with at least five purely indigenous Hausa Fulani Christian movements started by converts from Islam. Their stated life mission is to reach all Muslims for Christ.

Deliverance from Death

As we continue to work among Muslims, many who hold a militant ideology of death to every non-Muslim, the Lord has continued to miraculously deliver us from death. For example, God saved my life from the hands of a Muslim squadron leader in the Nigerian Air Force who fired his gun at me after putting it right against my temple. He was infuriated because I told him to go and arrest the Holy Spirit if he wanted to stop this great move of God that was taking place in northern Nigeria. The Lord jammed the chamber of his pistol as he pulled the trigger at point-blank range. Other officers present subdued the squadron leader, so he could not kill me. Truly the Lord has been good to us in the North!

THE POWER OF THE BEADS

The Muslim prayer beads are one very important feature of Islam that we all need to understand better. No good Muslim goes without his or her prayer beads, called chaplets, or rosaries. The Lord showed me in an elaborate revelation that these prayer beads are actually the altar from which all the spirits that serve the Islamic religion are released. The power and operation of the spirit of Islam are locked up in those beads. The beads are to the Muslims what enchantment stones are to animistic worshipers in traditional Nigerian religions. In order to see into the future, followers of Islam address the spirits by using these beads to invoke incantations and spells. The beads open up the doorway of access to the dark spirit realm.

Muslims use these beads as part of their prayer process and generally hold them in their hands throughout the day. If you observe closely, they are constantly chanting prayers under their breath, while they continuously roll each bead between their forefinger and thumb.

In the vision, God showed me that these beads represent an altar. It is the altar from which the spirits are released from the supernatural in order to attempt to shift the spiritual battle in their favor. This brings to mind Leviticus 6:13: "The fire must be kept burning on the altar continuously; it must not go out." We Christians need to understand that the spirit of Islam might well be subverting this biblical injunction in order to control and dominate the spirit realm day and night.

This spirit of Islam is radical and militant and oftentimes requires a blood sacrifice to satiate its perverse thirst. On many Fridays, Muslims venture into the streets chanting, *"Allahu Akabar, Allahu Akabar"* ("Allah is greatest, Allah is greatest"). Sometimes they carry placards, and other times they don't. Whether they do or not, this demonstration frequently ends in a bloody riot in which numerous Christians are murdered. Even when the stated reason for the riot is supposedly in protest toward Israel or America, it is the Nigerian Christians who end up being slaughtered and whose churches are burned down.

VICTORY AWAITING

God wants us to confront these forces of darkness by taking our place in Christ's resurrection power through the shed blood of Christ Jesus. We were told to ask the Lord to establish His throne in the midst of the followers of Islam during those riots according to Jeremiah 49:38 and 36 (in that order) and to destroy the spirit of Islam, who rules them. We need to take our stand and declare into being this Scripture:

> I will set Egyptians against Egyptians; everyone will fight against his brother, and everyone against his neighbor, city against city, kingdom against kingdom (Isa. 19:2).

The Church may be paying a heavy price, but it is also reaping an abundant harvest. Things are so much better now than they were just 10 years ago. Thank God for the faithful praying elders in Christian Association of Nigeria in the North. Thank God for the praying churches and for parachurch ministries like ours. Thank God for the prayers of the saints in other parts of the world. Thank God for the united voice of the Church in Nigeria over this issue. We do not yet have a full understanding of where He is taking us or why He has chosen us, but we are sure of this one thing: He is able to keep us until that glorious day of His coming and to keep that which we have committed into His hands.

CHAPTER TEN

KINGDOM PRINCIPLES FOR KINGDOM PROSPERITY

David Oyedepo

David Oyedepo, president and bishop of Living Faith Church Worldwide, is a dynamic leader of this multifaceted organization whose global impact cannot be overemphasized.

Through Bishop Oyedepo's insightful teachings on vision, economic empowerment, dominion and value-based leadership, many from Nigeria, as well as those from other nations of the world, have found fulfillment in pursuing their destinies. His life-transforming messages, published in over 70 books, keep generating amazing proof of financial, business and career success for men and women around the globe.

Oyedepo is also the president of World Mission Agency, an organization with branches in 30 African nations, where over 100,000 nationals from every facet of the workplace have been trained and equipped for effective leadership. These leadership-training programs have had steadily increasing influence for more than seven years across the continent of Africa.

David Oyedepo is the founding pastor of the ever growing congregation of Winners (a name used to refer to the church members) at the 50,400-seat Faith Tabernacle in Canaan Land, Ota, Nigeria. He is president of the newly founded Covenant University, designed to train 6,500 students from every African nation. He, his wife, Faith, and their children live in Lagos, Nigeria.

I will make you a great nation; I will bless you and make your name great; and you shall be a blessing.

G E N E S I S   1 2 : 2

In March 1981, I discovered a truth about prosperity that ended up destroying the poverty that plagued my life. At that time, I did not have a dime in a bank account anywhere! With my Bible and Gloria Copeland's book *God's Will Is Prosperity,* I embarked on a three-day adventure into the Word of God. On the third day, while I was reading, I got it! Light dawned from heaven like a flash of lightning! I jumped up and began to dance around the room with the excitement of my discovery! I came out and announced to everyone at the top of my voice, "I will never be poor!" It was a verdict backed up by light from heaven! And I believe that every demon in hell heard me! That day poverty ended in my life. I do not consider myself a preacher of prosperity, but I am a prophet. I knew without a doubt that God had given me a message for the Church.

Some time after that, I was in the United States attending a meeting, and God spoke to me specifically with these words: "Go back home and make My people rich!" Today, the manifestation of that word has become evident in our ministry: Because of the financial blessing God has given us, we are able to share the gospel of Jesus Christ with many others.

I was ministering in America some time ago, and a man, having enjoyed the time of ministry, walked up to me and asked, "What needs do you have in your ministry?" I said to him with absolute conviction, "Our ministry has no needs; we meet other people's needs!" To this day, we have not received a dime in aid from any other country in the world, nor have we ever solicited for it! Friends, it is not luck; it is not chance; it is light!

A MIRACLE FOR ALL TO SEE

Today, we have visitors from all over the globe. They marvel at the mighty work that God has done in our ministry. Our campus, Canaan Land, sits on over 630 acres of land in Ota, on the outskirts of Lagos, Nigeria. We have an elementary school, a middle school and a high school. Last year we opened our doors to 5,000 students at Covenant University (an affiliate of Oral Roberts University in Tulsa, Oklahoma). There is available housing for staff and guests of the ministry, as well as housing for professors and support staff of the university. We have a fleet of over 200 buses and numerous smaller vans to provide subsidized transportation between Lagos and Ota. To service these buses there is a full-service gas station. By the grace of God, we were able to build a 50,400-seat auditorium, Faith Tabernacle (the largest church auditorium in the world, which we also call Winners Chapel), where we hold our church services.

We also have our own publishing house, where every month we print 70,000 copies of books that I have authored. These books are distributed in Nigeria as well as in 30 other African countries. Over 4 million copies have been sold to date. The printing press is located on our nearby Capernaum campus, which itself is a testimony to the faithfulness of God. What makes all of this most remarkable is the fact that both of our campuses were constructed at a cost in excess of $500 million and they were paid for in cash. However, all of this did not happen overnight. It all began with an explosion of the revelation of prosperity in my heart many, many years ago. After that revelation, I knew I would never be the same again.

THE SEVEN PILLARS OF KINGDOM PROSPERITY

There is nothing God does without a reason. He said in Jeremiah 29:11 (*TEV*), "I alone know the plans I have for you." God is a planner. So, what is His plan, or reason, for blessing us? What are the Kingdom principles for Kingdom prosperity? Over the years, I have identified seven pillars, or strategies, of Kingdom prosperity. I will explain them.

Giving

In my years of ministry, I have come to realize that the level to which you are prepared to be a blessing is the level to which you will be blessed. Every blessing you receive must also flow out to others to enjoy, if you do not want the blessing to cease. Abraham's blessings were contingent on his obedience to the Lord, as well as on his faithfulness. If we want to experience the blessings of Abraham, we must cultivate Abraham's lifestyle. He was a constant giver. In Genesis 23, we read that Abraham needed a piece of land on which to bury his wife, Sarah. Though the people wanted to give it to him for free, he insisted on paying for it. His motive? To be a blessing to the people.

This reminds me of a time when someone gave me a parcel of land as a gift. I built a fence around it, erected two gates and gave it back to the person. Another person gave me a building in a reportedly good location (I never saw it). I sensed that this was a sacrificial gift on the woman's part and felt impressed by the

> *The level to which you are prepared to be a blessing is the level to which you will be blessed.*

Holy Spirit to bless her in return. I said to her, "It is in your heart to give this gift, but I seed it back to you the way Abraham seeded Isaac back to God on the altar. Like Isaac, your gift will not die but will multiply. Receive it back in Jesus' name."

As covenant people we should always be eager to bless. Here is an example: One day, I arrived at the church, and I saw our precious maintenance crew working hard. As I looked at them, I felt in my heart that some of them had personal financial needs, so I called their leader and asked him what he knew about them and their needs. I ended up giving a significant amount of money to take care of those needs. Why? Because, as Jesus said, "It is more blessed to give than to receive" (Acts 20:35).

God does not bless His people for the fun of it. He blesses primarily for His kingdom's sake. He blesses us so that we can be a blessing to others. When we stop being a blessing, we stop being blessed.

Our giving should be directed first to God and then to the people around us. God's love is a giving love. We take our example from John 3:16, which tells us that God so loved the world that He *gave* His best to the world—His Son, Jesus. God blessed Abraham, and Abraham responded by giving back to Him (see Gen. 14:18-20). He gave—he didn't just pray! He gave as if to say, "I receive the blessing, and this is my giving to demonstrate my love for You."

According to the Scriptures, having compassion for the poor and needy is lending to the Lord. When we reach out with compassion to the poor and the needy, God is committed to giving back to us, according to Matthew 10:40-42. We do not need a big bank account or deep pockets to bless those in need; all we need is a big heart.

Twenty years ago, I was a student worker in a remote village. When I arrived at the village, there was not a single church there! I said, "Lord, I must not leave this place the way it is, so help me in whichever way You will." I found a young man who spoke the language of the villagers and asked him to be my interpreter. I knew the work had begun!

First, I led the young man to the Lord. In 40 days, not only did we have a church in place, but we were also able to build a place for the church to meet. We built it with grass and other materials we could find locally, but God saw us as we painstakingly climbed the palm trees to cut down palm fronds for the roof. He also saw that when I left that village, I had less than when I had arrived. I had given away all of my shoes and clothes to the people there.

The day I left the village, the village chief came to church for the first time in his life! He said, "We have been told that anywhere the Church is established, civilization comes to that place.

Thank you for bringing civilization to our village." In the meantime, we had converts of all kinds in that church. Back then, I had not received a call to the ministry yet; I simply had a heart for giving to God's people. The oldest man on the village, on behalf of the entire village, presented a kerosene lamp to me, saying, "May the light you brought into our village continue to shine around the whole world through you." I believe that our present-day ministry was birthed from the seed that was sown in that village.

An essential form of giving is tithing, and it is one of the major keys to prosperity. Tithing is an inescapable covenant obligation. Prosperity is impossible when you do not give your tithe, because, according to Malachi 3:8-12, you come under a curse when you fail to give to God what rightfully belongs to Him. The tithe of our income does not belong to us but to God. If the tithe did not belong to God, He would not have said, "You have robbed Me" (Mal. 3:8). We have to understand that giving our tithe does not enrich God. It is entirely for our own benefit, as it secures our covenant of prosperity with God. In the same way that we pay our taxes to the government as our civic duty, we also have a covenant responsibility to give our tithe, as citizens of God's kingdom. The tithe is a transaction that guarantees us the opening of the windows of heaven.

Many years ago, I said to the Lord, "I don't have any cash to give as an offering. What am I going to do today? I have to give something!" I got out of bed very early that morning and went to the church to sweep it. That way, whatever would have been paid to whoever had the responsibility of sweeping the church would be my offering to God. Sometimes we may not have any cash to give, but there are always other creative ways to give to the Lord.

When we began our church plant, we had a great need for money, but the offerings that we received were inadequate. As I discussed the matter with God, He said to me, "Son, give me your car." I knew without a doubt that it was God speaking to me. When I told my wife, she simply said, "Praise the Lord." That was it! I called one of my staff members and asked him to drive the car back to the car dealer. I was so excited because I felt privileged that the Lord had asked it of me. Shortly after that, I heard the Lord say to me "My son, David, even if you did not want to be rich, it is too late now!" God made a promise to me the way He did to Abraham in Genesis 22.

It is important to note here that not every sacrifice is acceptable to God. *We must give cheerfully, with a willing heart, or we might as well not give at all.* We do not do God a favor when we give to Him. There is a blessing in giving cheerfully and willingly, and it becomes ours!

Working

The Bible says, "Unless the LORD builds the house, they labor in vain who build it; unless the LORD guards the city, the watchman stays awake in vain." (Ps. 127:1). This means that there is labor involved in establishing the house that God builds. God blesses the work of our hands as long as we intend it for His glory. Giving and working go hand in hand. Giving procures the blessing, while working opens the channel through which that blessing flows to us. When we give, we must work to create channels for the blessing. In the same manner, when we work, we must give—otherwise we will cheat ourselves of the blessing. Many of us have been taught how to give, but we have not been taught the place and the dignity of labor. The Bible also says in 2 Thessalonians 3:10 that he who does not work should not eat.

When I first started preaching the prosperity message, I was the object of ridicule, because I did not look like I was living what I preached. However, I kept working and doing what God had charged me to do—despite the outburst of criticism that was directed against me. However, I trusted in the God in whom I believed. I was called every conceivable derogatory name back then, but today the fulfillment of the vision speaks for itself. I hear those names no longer.

Abraham was a hard worker. At the age of 75, he was still tending to his livestock. Isaac, following the example of his father's work ethic, dug a well for water. Isaac's detractors fought with him over the well. He dug another well only to be fought with again. He dug a third well and finally wore out his enemies (see Gen. 26). Jacob, keeping with family tradition, was also a hard worker—and a smart one. He outwitted his father-in-law, Laban, who had hoped to keep him in perpetual servitude. Laban agreed with Jacob's request to get all the speckled cattle in the flock (an infrequent and rare occurrence), and Jacob devised an ingenious way to multiply the number of speckled calves (see Gen. 30:37-43). Our fathers in the faith worked hard, tirelessly and creatively. Whatever work we do determines the fruit of our increase. No matter what that work is, as long as it is coupled with giving, it will produce increase.

Applying Wisdom

Thinking and applying our God-given intellect to the pursuit of financial productivity is essential to success. Thinking, in this context, is the ability to coordinate thoughts productively for increased output. When Paul talked about "the eyes of your understanding being enlightened" in Ephesians 1:18, he was referring to being mentally sound—not doing ordinary thinking, but producing high-level productive ideas. When we think the way the world thinks, we get what the world gets. The economy of the country does not determine our prosperity. Our prosperity is determined by how we think about and respond to the Word of God! God's principles do not change, regardless of the state of the national economy.

For "who has known the mind of the LORD that he may instruct Him?" But we have the mind of Christ (1 Cor. 2:16).

If we have the mind of Christ and if He is the wisdom of God by which all things are created, then we are by inheritance possessors of divine creativity. It is our birthright to operate in the creative realms of God. The world should pay attention to us as it did to Jesus when He walked the earth. However, the world will never take notice of us until we produce the kind of results that Jesus did in order to command the world's attention and respect.

Trusting in God

It is one thing to know God and another thing to trust Him. The realm of trusting is the realm of continuous triumph. Many of us trust in our paychecks, in other people and even in ourselves, but we struggle with trusting God.

Thus says the Lord: "Cursed is the man that trusts in man and makes flesh his strength, whose heart departs from the LORD" (Jer. 17:5).

My trust is not in the congregation I pastor, as I do not do my planning based on the size of the congregation. I plan based on my knowledge of God. From the day that I had a revelation of the phrase "Woe unto him that trusts in man," I determined that I would avoid woe. Contrary to the "wise" counsel of the great economists and financial advisers of our day, I am not putting away money for my children to spend tomorrow. I am teaching them today the principles of how to possess their own wealth and prosper in God's will.

Since God has successfully managed the entire universe up to this point without our help and investment, surely He can manage our lives! All He requires is that we trust Him.

Waiting for God's Timing

> For when God made a promise to Abraham, because He could swear by no one greater, He swore by Himself, saying, "Surely blessing I will bless you, and multiplying I will multiply you." And so, after he had patiently endured, he obtained the promise (Heb. 6:13-15).

God made a promise to Abraham, yet Abraham needed patience to witness the fulfillment of that promise. The covenant of prosperity is not a magic wand but an adventure of faith. In Habakkuk 2:3, God said every vision is for an appointed time, so though it tarries, wait for it.

Quick prosperity will almost always produce grievous consequences, because it lacks the required foundation for lasting results—God's timing.

In 1981, God spoke to me, saying, "The hour has come to liberate the world from the oppression of the devil, through the preaching of the word of faith." That was God's revelation to me of the birthing of a ministry that would have a worldwide impact. The direct mandate to begin that ministry and spread the Word to the rest of Africa did not come until 1994—13 years later! There is usually a waiting period between when the Lord gives the word and the fruition of the promise. Quick prosperity will almost always produce grievous consequences, because it lacks the required foundation for lasting results.

We must not become weary and give up before the promise is fulfilled, because there is a "due season" (Gal. 6:9). If we remain resolute in our commitment to see the promise fulfilled, when that season comes, we will reap our harvest; but if we faint, we will fall. In a world that is in as much of a hurry as it is today—a world that wants instant gratification—we need an understanding of God that will help us see beyond this system.

It has often been said that it takes a lot of discipline to wait, but God is never late. It is the blessings of God, not the blessings of material possessions, that make us rich and add no sorrows to our life. Do not look for shortcuts. Wait for God's timing.

Speaking in Faith

Speaking is the sixth pillar of kingdom prosperity. Whatever we are not able to speak by faith, we have not believed:

And since we have the same spirit of faith, according to what is written, "I believed and therefore I spoke," we also believe and therefore speak (2 Cor. 4:13).

In the realm of the spirit, our words are what give expression to our choices. God sees what we say as the conclusion to our expectation. When the children of Israel were about to enter the land flowing with milk and honey and they said, "We are not able to go up and possess the land," God said to them, through Moses and Aaron, "Say to them, 'As I live,' says the LORD, 'just as you have spoken in my hearing, so I will do to you'" (Num. 14:28).

Prosperity must become our language, in private as well as in public. We make our way prosperous by giving (provokes divine blessings), by working (provides the channel for the blessings to flow), by applying wisdom with our intellect (enhances greater results), by trusting (without which the blessings are not delivered into our hands) and by waiting (because we need patience to see fruit grow from what we have planted); and then prosperity comes into our house by speaking in faith.

There is a difference between talking prosperity and bragging. Talking prosperity is giving expression to our stand in God, making it our lifestyle.

Giving Thanks

Thanksgiving is the seventh strategy toward achieving biblical prosperity. Abraham gave glory to God, and that opened the channel for his miracle (see Rom. 4:20). He was thankful to God even before he saw the manifestation of what he was trusting God to provide. To be thankful is to be fruitful. The opposite is also true: to be thankless is to be fruitless. It is the giving of thanks and praise that ultimately provokes the increase.

In the miracle of the feeding of the 5,000, Jesus gave thanks for the five loaves of bread and two fish, which multiplied and fed 5,000 men plus women and children; and Jesus' disciples collected 12 baskets of leftovers. There was no multiplication until Jesus gave thanks to the Father in anticipation of the miracle of provision.

Giving, working, applying wisdom, trusting and waiting represent planting the seed, while speaking and giving thanks represent watering the seed.

A WORD OF CAUTION

I have one word of caution as we study the biblical truth of prosperity. One mistake that many of us make at some point or another is to think of God as our heavenly banker. He is not that; He is our heavenly Father.

GOD'S WORD—THE SEED OF PROSPERITY

Prosperity in the kingdom of God is predicated on the platform of encounters with the Bible. The Word of God is God's highway to the world of wealth. Our encounters with God's commandments make us commanders. We can command sickness at will, because we have encountered the Word of healing. By the same token, we can command wealth because we have encountered the Word of prosperity.

Jesus said,

> The Spirit of the LORD is upon Me, because He has anointed Me to preach the gospel to the poor (Luke 4:18).

What do we do to the poor? We preach the gospel. And what is good news to the poor? Prosperity! What is good news to the hungry? Prosperity! What is good news to the naked? Prosperity! What is good news to the homeless? Prosperity!

Prosperity is preached, not prayed! You don't fast to get prosperity; rather, you teach the principles of the Word of God. The encounters that cause faith to rise in you come by exposure to the Word, not by the rigors of religious exercise.

FAITH AND OBEDIENCE—OUR COVENANT ACCESS

> But without faith it is impossible to please Him (Heb. 11:6).

> But the just shall live by his faith (Hab. 2:4).

How does God bless? you ask. Well, according to the Scriptures, it is in obeying the "law of the farm." It is in realizing that there is a time to plant and a time to harvest: "While the earth remains, seedtime and harvest . . . shall not cease" (Gen. 8:22).

"Seed" is not exclusively a reference to money. In this context, it primarily represents the Word of God. While God's Word opens us up to prosperity, our faith in His Word is what makes it real. In other words, God's Word is the covenant platform for our prosperity, and faith is our covenant access into that prosperity.

Faith is not saying, "I agree." That is consent. Faith is not mental assent. It is an active living force that controls your attitude and your actions as you allow the Word you have encountered to direct and control you. For instance, Malachi 3:10 says,

> "Bring all the tithes into the storehouse, that there may be food in My house, and try Me now in this," says the LORD of hosts, "If I will not open for you the windows of heaven and pour out for you such blessing that there will not be room enough to receive it."

If all you do when you read this verse is thank God for the message but withhold the tithe because you have other pressing bills, or you grumble as you give your offerings (from your leftover change), then you certainly don't have a revelation of faith. Faith is an active living force! When faith lives in individuals, it illuminates the power of the Scriptures.

Abraham, first known as Abram, understood this principle well. Called to a strange land, he was faithful and obedient to the command of the Lord, and as a result he received a blessing that he had done nothing to earn. His prosperity was recorded for all of posterity to witness: "Abram was very rich in livestock, in silver, and in gold" (Gen. 13:2). Abraham was rich, simply because he acted on the Word of God! He received the Word; he applied himself to fulfilling it; and he prospered!

Faith is invaluable in other areas of our lives as well. I came home one day, and my wife sadly announced to me, "I had a miscarriage." I said to her, "That cannot happen. What's for dinner?" That was the final word spoken on that issue. No further discussion was necessary. No long, drawn-out prayer was offered, and I gave my wife no further opportunity for explanations. I did this not because I was insensitive but because I had a revelation from God concerning the power of faith. The result? No miscarriage! The pregnancy was sustained by the sheer force of faith and produced our first son, David Jr.! For "this is the victory that has overcome the world—our faith" (1 John 5:4).

The connection between faith and covenant wealth is simply obedience; that is, walking in obedience to what the covenant demands. When we walk in practical obedience to the terms of the covenant, we walk in faith; and it will always bring God's blessings to us. Consequently, obedience will inevitably lead to prosperity.

If they obey and serve Him, they shall spend their days in prosperity, and their years in pleasures (Job 36:11).

CHAPTER ELEVEN

PREPARING A PEOPLE FOR GREAT WORKS

Enoch A. Adeboye with Eskor Mfon

One of the most humble and unassuming men you will ever meet, Enoch Adeboye holds a doctoral degree in applied mathematics (hydrodynamics). A former professor at the University of Lagos, he gave up teaching to go into full-time ministry in 1981, when he was appointed the general overseer of the prestigious Redeemed Christian Church of God (RCCG).

Adeboye is known for his clear and easy-to-understand teaching style, and he is in great demand worldwide as a speaker. His ministry and his teaching, which focus on holiness, are often followed by a demonstration of signs and wonders. There are numerous documented testimonies of miraculous healings occurring as he ministers.

A man of prayer, Adeboye hosts the annual Holy Ghost Congress of the RCCG, where millions of people gather to worship and praise God. He secludes himself to fast and pray for at least two weeks prior to this annual event, seeking fresh direction from the Lord.

His ministry is not only characterized by prayer but also by strong, dynamic leadership. Numerous well-established Christian leaders in Nigeria—leaders in church ministry, in the marketplace and in government—consider Pastor Adeboye their spiritual father and constantly seek his counsel and wisdom on various matters.

Affectionately referred to as "Daddy G.O." (for "general overseer"), Pastor Adeboye is married to his wonderful wife, Folu, or "Mummy G.O." Their children are grown.

Eskor Mfon

An incredibly resourceful and visionary leader, Pastor Eskor Mfon wears numerous hats. In addition to serving as the senior pastor of the RCCG parish City of David, one of the most dynamic churches in Lagos, he also serves as state pastor for Lagos State 3A District.

With an academic background in marketing, Eskor worked for many years as a client service director with one of the largest advertising agencies in Nigeria. He currently runs his own successful advertising agency, providing services to a cross section of the emerging Nigerian industrial market.

Eskor is known as a shepherd with a tender heart toward his flock. A man of prayer, he has been known to respond to emergencies at all hours of the night in order to pray with or encourage people who are struggling. His passion to see the downtrodden and hurting effectively ministered to led him to begin an extensive feeding program aptly named A CAN Can Make a Difference.

Located in the affluent Victoria Island area of Lagos, Eskor's church serves as church home to many of the top leaders in government, the military and the business world. His passion is to ensure that the vision of the RCCG leaves a lasting legacy for the posterity of Nigeria and indeed Africa. He, his wife, Bimpe, and their children live in Lagos.

The year was 1981, and unknown to me (Enoch Adeboye) at the time, I was about to begin a journey that would lead to the most incredible adventure of my life. I had just been elected to take over the reins of leadership of the Redeemed Christian Church of God (RCCG). At the time, there were 42 local church branches, which we call parishes, scattered primarily over the southern part of Nigeria. As we celebrated the occasion with joyous festivities and prayers, I could not help but wonder what was in store for me. But I am getting ahead of myself, as the story did not begin in 1981.

THE CHURCH'S FOUNDING

In 1952, Josiah Akindayomi, an uneducated man born into an idol-worshiping family, experienced a miraculous call to begin a church. He had become a Christian in 1927 through contact with Church Missionary Society. One day, in a vision, God gave Josiah—fondly known to members of the RCCG as "Pa" Akindayomi—the name of the church he was being mandated to begin. Though he could neither read nor write, in the vision he saw what he thought were strange symbols appear on a wall. He was instructed to copy down what he saw, which he painstakingly copied onto a wooden board. He took the board with him to the home of some of his relatives in Lagos who read out the name: Redeemed Christian Church of God. On hearing that this was the name the Lord had instructed him to give the church, his family mocked and derided him. Undaunted, he further disclosed that in the vision, God had told him that this church would spread to the ends of the earth and would still be serving faithfully when the Lord returned to the earth in the Second Coming.

Amidst this derisive atmosphere and with very little education, Josiah embarked on his commission to change the world. With tremendous signs and wonders, the church grew in leaps and bounds; and Josiah became the first general superintendent, or, later, general overseer, of the RCCG. He was supernaturally taught to read the Bible in his native Yoruba language, and it soon became clear to all that he was a truly anointed leader. His gifts of preaching, healing, prophecy and the working of miracles caused the church to expand rapidly. Pa Akindayomi died in 1980 at the age of 71, leaving behind a legacy that endures to this day.

TRANSFER OF LEADERSHIP

In the early 1970s, I was well into my career as a professor of mathematics (specializing in hydrodynamics) at one of the leading universities in Nigeria. I joined the RCCG, and before long, I was asked to be the interpreter for Pa Akindayomi, translating his messages from Yoruba to English. It was this close interaction with him that seemed to indicate to everyone that I would be his natural successor to lead the church. Sure enough, after my mentor went to be with the Lord, I was named general overseer of the RCCG.

When I assumed leadership, I realized that one of the first orders of business would be to cast the vision for the ministry. By so doing, we could then begin to develop leaders who could move ahead with that vision in order to maintain and accelerate the growth of the church. The following became the vision statement for the RCCG:

- To make it to heaven
- To take as many people to heaven as possible with us

- To make holiness our lifestyle
- To plant a church of the RCCG within five minutes of every home worldwide

God has made it abundantly clear to us that our primary mission is to make it to heaven and to take as many people as possible with us. These two stated goals gave birth to the rest of our vision. Since the Scriptures teach that without holiness no one will see God (see Heb. 12:14), we are committed to living a lifestyle of holiness, as taught by the Scriptures. In order to fulfill our goal of taking as many people to heaven with us as possible (see Acts 1:8) and recognizing that in certain parts of the world people don't have the means to travel great distances to church, we are committed to planting churches within easy reach of every person.

The primary role of the churches we plant the world over is to disciple people as we lead them to the Lord. We believe that planting churches is a means to fulfilling the mandate of making disciples of all nations. In light of the magnitude of our

Our primary mission is to make it to heaven and to take as many people as possible with us.

vision and because of the large number of people that we are constantly discipling, we encourage everyone to be involved in ministry. We believe that everyone is basically called to "do the work of an evangelist" (2 Tim. 4:5). We therefore utilize a large number of volunteers in our ministry as well as a large number of local church pastors who are also professionals in the workplace.

In our pastoral ranks globally, we have attorney generals, lawyers, doctors, engineers, architects, CEOs, marketing and advertising executives, as well as many other professionals.

God desires to use every believer in the workplace to fulfill the mandate of ministry.

This allows us a better understanding of the workplace environment and consequently provides a platform for our voice to be heard there.

MODEL PARISHES

As part of our mission to have a global impact, we began setting up what came to be known as model parishes of the RCCG. These are local assemblies geared toward reaching educated professionals, entrepreneurs and leaders in government and politics. Prior to this, the church was made up largely of the poor and the uneducated. These model parishes grew rapidly, as they appealed to the influential educated elite; and soon we established two new districts, separate from the classical arm of the RCCG. These districts are known as the Apapa Family and the Ikeja Family. They have the responsibility of overseeing the administration of all our model parishes.

Before long, church members belonging to the Apapa Family and the Ikeja Family began establishing new churches both inside and outside of Nigeria. Born out of my belief that God desires to use every believer in the workplace to fulfill the mandate of ministry, I would encourage those who were traveling abroad for any reason to consider planting a branch of the RCCG in the area to which the Lord was sending them.

This is how our mission work started, but it didn't end there. Every church plant desired to reach out and build more new churches, and they have. This is how the RCCG began to multiply across entire cities and nations. For example, in the United States alone we now have over 150 parishes, with new ones springing up on a monthly basis. There are approximately 6,000 RCCG churches in over 50 nations today, and we continue to spread and reach out into areas that would ordinarily be hard for foreign missionaries to venture into.

CITY OF DAVID

Among the model parishes in Nigeria that have made significant inroads into impacting the more educated, as well as sending out missionaries to plant churches in other nations, is City of David, located on Victoria Island in Lagos.

I will ask Pastor Eskor Mfon of City of David to tell this part of the story.

Gaining Momentum

With a new, clearly defined mandate and a strong crop of educated, dynamic visionaries stepping into pastoral roles, RCCG model parishes began to gain momentum. Recognizing the great need for reinventing the Nigerian socioeconomic infrastructure and restoring the beleaguered middle class, many of our churches have extended their ministry into the workplace.

The primary motivation for this is the knowledge that the church is meant to be more than just a gathering of people on Sunday and certainly much more than a four-wall enclosure where we worship God. Our people in the workplace believe that they are engaged in valid, God-ordained ministry seven days a week.

At City of David (COD), for example, we have established an elementary school, middle school and high school that base their teaching on a Christian worldview. We have also set up a hospital and a bank to serve the local communities in order to provide medical care for the poor and loans for potential business owners. At the time of this writing, COD is in the process of obtaining a radio license in order to establish our own Christian radio station, and we also are setting up our own publishing house.

Feeding the Hungry

In addition to all of this, COD, in conjunction with Reverend Joe Olaiya (the author of chapter 5), has embarked on an ambitious feeding program named A CAN Can Make a Difference. Every Sunday, 30,000 destitute people in over 20 locations in the city of Lagos are fed hot meals. Doctors and nurses are on hand at all of these locations to provide free medical services to those who need medical care. If necessary, the people are taken to the COD hospital, House of Hope, where they are cared for at no cost to them.

The feeding program has been extended into the prisons in Lagos, where prisoners often do not get three meals a day, not to mention a single hot meal. With the help of Joe Olaiya, we have also extended the program into the largely Muslim North of Nigeria. It is the ultimate goal of COD to spread this program to every state in Nigeria so that every single person who desires a meal is fed at least one hot meal a day. An ambitious venture, I hear you say. Well, with God nothing shall be impossible.

It is for this reason that COD is in the process of purchasing a large farm that will provide the volume of food necessary to ensure the rapid expansion of the feeding program. Growing most of our own food will dramatically reduce the colossal cost of providing meals for as many people as we plan to feed.

Doing It for Jesus

Why, you may ask, are you interested in feeding the poor and providing health care for the destitute and the homeless? Because the Bible says, "Pure and undefiled religion before God and the Father is this: to visit orphans and widows in their trouble" (Jas. 1:27). Jesus said, "For I was hungry and you gave Me food; I was thirsty and you gave Me drink" (Matt. 25:35). Jesus taught that whatever we do for the least of these we are doing for Him (see Matt. 25:40). It is so much easier for people to believe you when you tell them that Jesus loves them, after you have reached out to them in love and have filled their hungry bellies.

We are motivated by the love of God and compelled by the needs of the people around us. Consider these statistics regarding Africa:

- Every night, 800 million people go to bed hungry.
- Approximately 200 million children under the age of five don't have enough food.
- Every day, 13,500 children die from pneumonia, diarrhea, malaria or measles.
- Every day, more than 30,000 children die from preventable hunger and disease.
- 30 million infants lack routine, lifesaving vaccinations.
- 80 percent of children under the age of 15 that are infected with HIV are children living in Africa.
- Every day, 6,500 Africans die from AIDS.[1]

With these types of statistics, how can we sit on the sidelines, doing nothing, and yet pretend that our Christianity is effective?

AFRICA MISSIONS NORTH AMERICA

With this overwhelming crisis of poverty and hunger sweeping across our continent, which Pastor Eskor has just described, the RCCG in North America is poised to help combat this insidious problem. The RCCG has established its Africa Missions North America (AMNA) program geared toward

- focused intervention for greater impact,
- strengthing and supporting community systems,
- leadership empowerment,
- sustainability and stewardship.

Times of crisis present the Body of Christ with unprecedented opportunities. The Church must rise to meet the challenges, because as hurting people experience the love of God through the Body of Christ, hearts are transformed and lives are changed so that people become more productive. In communities across the continent of Africa, the Church should—indeed the Church *must*—play a leading role in transforming communities for Christ by reaching out with the love of God through whatever means are at our disposal. For AMNA, the avenues we feel led to work through are education, health care, HIV/AIDS education and treatment, food aid, microenterprise development, humanitarian assistance, leadership development and child care.

THE GOSPEL OF THE KINGDOM

We like to think that the RCCG is a well-rounded ministry, covering the needs of spirit, soul and body—in other words, a ministry that reaches out to the total person. We believe that for social transformation to happen, we must be involved in meeting material as well as spiritual needs. Jesus fed the 5,000 both spiritually and physically in order that His message would have the desired impact. While we are deeply engaged in different programs that

For social transformation to happen, the Church must be involved in meeting material as well as spiritual needs.

provide health care, food and education to many, we are also focused on reaching millions with the truth of God's Word, which provides hope for the future. This is the gospel of the Kingdom.

RIVERS OF LIVING WATER

The atmosphere is festive, and there is an excited buzz among the crowd. They seem undaunted by the heat, and there is clear anticipation among the people about what God is going to do. Over the next seven days, there will be roughly 6 to 7 million people who will gather together in an open field at the RCCG campground facilities (Redemption City), located at kilometer 46 along the Lagos-Ibadan expressway. The occasion? The annual Holy Ghost Congress of the RCCG.

The Holy Ghost Congress began with Lekki '98 at Lekki Beach on the outskirts of Lagos. The initial gathering attracted a crowd estimated at over 6 million people. The annual Holy Ghost Congress, held every December, is an outgrowth of the Holy Ghost Service, held on the first Friday of every month. The

Holy Ghost Service is an all-night prayer meeting that includes a healing and miracle service, at which the average attendance is over 500,000 people. As it has grown in popularity because of the hunger of the people and their desire to press deeper into God, we have honored requests to hold similar meetings in many other countries. We currently hold Holy Ghost Services in South Africa, the United Kingdom, France, Germany, Switzerland and Denmark, among others.

Guests from well over 50 nations attend the annual Holy Ghost Congress. Many of them have been overwhelmed at the sheer magnitude of the crowds and the tremendous praise and worship that rises up from the people. Lee Grady, the editor of *Charisma* magazine, attended the Congress in 2001. Lee attempted to walk through the crowd, but he gave up after walking for 30 minutes and barely making it to the middle.

JEHOVAH JIREH—OUR PROVIDER

With the magnitude of this annual celebration of worship, you may wonder how such an event is funded. No doubt, the expense involved with hosting such an event is significant, costing approximately $10 million when all is said and done. The miracle is that God always provides for us in spite of the fact that the RCCG does not have a centralized bank account. When we have a project, we present it to the Lord saying, "Lord, we believe that you inspired this project. If that is truly the case, then make provision for all that we need." He has never failed to provide for our needs. We constantly rely on Him to multiply our provision in the same way that He multiplied the five loaves of bread and two fish and fed 5,000 people.

In the United States, we host an annual RCCG North American Convention. There is an attendance of approximately 7,000 RCCG members at that convention, costing over $500,000 to host. As we continue to plan for the rapid growth and expansion of our ministry in North America, the RCCG has also acquired a sizable parcel of land near Dallas, Texas. There are plans to construct a retreat center, a Christian holiday resort and a youth camp on the property. Two hundred fifty acres have already been paid for and negotiations to purchase another 250 to 300 acres continue. Similar activity is occurring in other countries around the world as the RCCG continues to fulfill our God-breathed mandate to plant a church within five minutes of every person.

It is astounding to see how the Lord has faithfully continued to meet our needs. Over all, the RCCG worldwide accumulates annual expenses in the rather extraordinary amount of several hundred million dollars. This funding is all provided by Nigerian believers who give faithfully to the vision.

PRAYER—THE KEY

How is it that we are able to do so much and fund such huge expenses without a centralized financial office? Well, there is no doubt in my mind that prayer is the key to the continued success of our ministry. Prayer is the natural outcome of a total surrender to God, knowing full well that you can do nothing without Him. We believe that what might take a person a whole year to figure out and implement can be achieved in 10 minutes on one's knees, waiting on God in prayer. We have chosen to take God at His word and are convinced that Jesus meant what He said when He called us to be like Him. We are convinced that signs and wonders should follow believers as a sign to the unbeliever that our God is alive and well and that He is interested in the affairs of all human beings.

The ability to walk in the miraculous carries tremendous responsibility along with it. In order for us to be prepared to shoulder this responsibility, we are constantly in prayer. As we pray, we find that we allow more of God and less of ourselves to be seen as we do the work of ministry. As we see literal miracles manifest themselves in our ministry, we are under no illusions about the fact that the miracles have nothing to do with us and everything to do with Him. There are documented cases of healings, raisings from the dead and the restoration of atrophied limbs, among numerous other miracles. The greatest miracle of all, however, is the miracle of salvation, as millions of people in our nation and around the globe continue to turn to the Lord as a result of our ministry to them. While the reports of the miraculous may be new to some believers in other parts of the world, we have been seeing such miracles for many, many years.

No Limits with God

We are in awe of what the Lord has begun to do in our midst, and what is even more astounding is the fact that He has only just begun. Truly, He takes the foolish things of the world to confound the wise. It seems almost laughable that God would choose to raise up Africans—more specifically, Nigerians—and send them out as missionaries to the very nations that brought the gospel message to us initially. But God is sovereign in His dealings with us, and He is certainly at liberty to move however and among whomever He chooses.

In the words of one great man of God, "The world is yet to see what God can do through a man who fully surrenders to Him." If we will only surrender to Him completely, giving our lives as living sacrifices, then there is no limit to what God will do through us.

ENDNOTES

Introduction

1. David B. Barrett and Todd M. Johnson, *World Christian Encyclopedia* (Pasadena, CA: William Carey Library, 2001), p. 8.
2. David B. Barrett, "Status of Global Mission 2000," *International Bulletin of Missionary Research* (January 2002), p. 23.

Chapter One

1. "Nigeria," *Lonely Planet World Guide*, 2003. http://www.lonelyplanet.com/destinations/africa/nigeria/ (accessed July 9, 2003).
2. "Nigeria," *1Up Info*, June 1991. http://www.1upinfo.com/country-guide-study/nigeria/nigeria11.html (accessed July 9, 2003).
3. Ibid.
4. Minna Song, "The Biafran War," *African Postcolonial Literature in English*, 1989. http://www.scholars.nus.edu.sg/post/nigeria/biafra.html (accessed July 9, 2003).
5. "Nigeria," *1Up Info*, June 1991.
6. "Nigeria," *1Up Info*, June 1991.
7. "Images of Festac 77," *Centre for Black and African Arts and Civilization*, 2002. http://www.cbaac.org/images_festac.htm (accessed July 9, 2003).

8. Joseph Okpaku, Sr., *The Arts and Civilization of Black and African Peoples,* vol. 8, quoted in "Images of Festac 77," *Centre for Black and African Arts and Civilization,* 2002. http://www.cbaac.org/images_festac.htm (accessed July 9, 2003).
9. Max Lucado, *When God Whispers Your Name* (Dallas: Word Publishing, 1994), pp. 103-104

Chapter Eleven

1. Statistics compiled from World Relief by Tayo Fagbenro in a business development profile commissioned by Africa Missions North America.

More Ways to Grow Closer to God

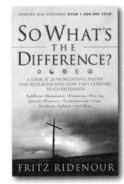
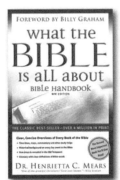
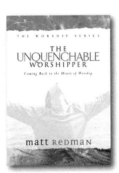

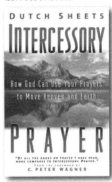

More of the Best from C. Peter Wagner

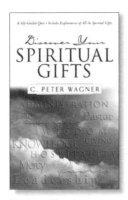
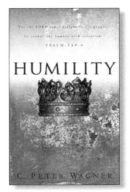

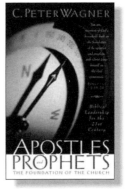